Data Science for Beginners

Introduction

Preface

Module 1: Introduction to Data Science

Unit 1 - Understanding the importance of data science in everyday life
Unit 2 - Introduction to basic data concepts and terminology

Module 2: Data Collection and Analysis

Unit 1 - Learning methods of data collection
Unit 2 - Introduction to data types and data structures
Unit 3 - Hands-on exercises in collecting and organizing data
Unit 4 - Basic data analysis techniques using graphs and charts

Module 3: Introduction to Programming

Unit 1 - Basic concepts of programming using Python
Unit 2 - Introduction to coding environments like Jupyter Notebooks
Unit 3 - Writing simple scripts to manipulate and analyze data

Module 4: Data Visualization

Unit 1 - Understanding the importance of data visualization
Unit 2 - Introduction to visualization libraries like Matplotlib and Seaborn

Module 5: Machine Learning Basics

Unit 1 - Introduction to machine learning concepts
Unit 2 - Understanding supervised and unsupervised learning

Module 6: Big Data and Data Engineering

Unit 1 - Introduction to big data concepts and technologies
Unit 2 - Understanding data storage and retrieval systems
Unit 3 - Exploring distributed computing frameworks like Hadoop and Spark

Module 7: Ethical Considerations in Data Science

Unit 1 - Discussing ethical considerations in data collection and analysis
Unit 2 - Understanding bias and fairness in machine learning models
Unit 3 - Encouraging responsible use of data and algorithms

Module 8: Quiz Time

    Quiz
    Answers

Module 9: The Historical Evolution of Data Science

Module 10: Fun Facts about Data Science

A story to get motivated from

Potential Breakthroughs

Glossary

Conclusion

Introduction

The Dawn of a New Era

Hello, dear reader! My name is Nitin, and I am thrilled to welcome you to this exciting journey into the world of data science. With nearly two decades of experience in IT, I've seen firsthand how the power of data can transform businesses and lives. But this book is not just about my professional experiences – it's also a personal journey that involves my family, particularly my wonderful wife, Richa, and our bright, curious daughter, Vaanya.

A Family Affair

Let me start with a story that brings the importance of data science into the realm of our everyday lives. One sunny afternoon, as I was engrossed in a project on my laptop, Vaanya came running to me with a question: "Papa, how does my favorite cartoon know what episodes I like the most?" At first, I was taken aback by the complexity of her question, but then I realized it was a perfect opportunity to introduce her to the fascinating world of data science.

As we sat down together, I explained how her viewing habits created data that the streaming service analyzed to recommend new episodes she might enjoy. Her eyes widened with wonder, and it was at that moment I knew I wanted to write this book – to demystify data science for young minds and show them the incredible possibilities that data holds.

Bridging the Gap

The world is evolving at an unprecedented pace, and data is at the heart of this transformation. From predicting consumer behavior to optimizing supply chains, data science is revolutionizing industries across the globe. However, the terminology and concepts can often seem daunting, especially for beginners. My goal with this book is to bridge that gap, making data science accessible, engaging, and fun for readers of all ages.

Why This Book?

Having worked across various domains and seen the impact of data firsthand, I believe that understanding data science is no longer optional – it's essential. Whether you're a student, a professional looking to upskill, or simply curious about the subject, this book is designed for you. With real-life examples, hands-on exercises, and a sprinkle of wit, we'll embark on an adventure that will change the way you perceive data.

Setting the Stage

Before we dive into the specifics, let's set the stage for what's to come. This book is structured to gradually build your understanding of data science, starting with the basics and progressing to more advanced topics. We'll begin with an introduction to key concepts and terminology, explore real-life applications, and then delve into hands-on projects that will allow you to apply what you've learned.

Preface

A Personal Journey into Data Science

As I sit down to write this preface, I am filled with a sense of excitement and anticipation. Reflecting on my IT, I realize how integral data has been to every step of my professional journey. But it's not just my career that has been shaped by data – my personal life, especially my experiences with my wife, Richa, and our daughter, Vaanya, have been deeply intertwined with the world of data science.

The Spark of Curiosity

It all started with a simple question from Vaanya, a moment that many parents might recognize. She was curious about how her favorite streaming service knew her preferences. This innocent question sparked a profound realization in me – the importance of understanding data and its implications from an early age. I wanted to equip her and others like her, with the knowledge to navigate and leverage this data-driven world.

The Vision Behind the Book

This book is not just a technical manual or a textbook. It is a labor of love, a culmination of years of experience, and a desire to make data science accessible and enjoyable for everyone. My vision is to demystify data science, to strip away the jargon, and to present it in a way that is engaging, relatable, and practical. Whether you're a young student, a seasoned professional, or a curious learner, my hope is that this book will inspire you to see data science not just as a field of study, but as a lens through which to view and understand the world.

The Importance of Data Literacy

In today's world, data literacy is as important as traditional literacy. We are surrounded by data – from the smart devices we use to the social media platforms we engage with, and the services we consume. Understanding data, how it's collected, analyzed, and interpreted, is crucial for making informed decisions, both in our personal and professional lives. This book aims to provide you with the foundational knowledge and skills to become data literate, to think critically about data, and to harness its power for good.

A Family Endeavor

Writing this book has been a family endeavor. Richa has been my constant support, providing invaluable insights and feedback, and keeping me grounded throughout the process. Vaanya's curiosity and enthusiasm have been a continuous source of inspiration. Together, we have explored the wonders of data science, learning and growing along the way. This book is a testament to our collective journey, and it is my hope that it will ignite the same sense of wonder and curiosity in you.

What to Expect

The journey through this book is designed to be a blend of learning and fun. We'll start with the basics – understanding what data is, and why it matters. We'll explore real-life applications of data science, from healthcare and finance to entertainment and environmental conservation. Along the way, we'll delve into key concepts and terminology, breaking them down into digestible, easy-to-understand pieces.

But we won't stop there. This book is also packed with hands-on exercises and practical examples that will allow you to apply what you've learned. Whether it's creating your own data visualizations or building simple predictive models, you'll get to experience the thrill of working with data firsthand.

A Note on the Writing Style

You'll notice that this book is written in a conversational, engaging style. I believe that learning should be enjoyable, and I've made every effort to infuse the text with humor, anecdotes, and real-life stories to keep you engaged. After all, data science is not just about numbers and algorithms – it's about people, stories, and the impact data can have on our lives.

Final Thoughts

As we embark on this journey together, I want you to know that this book is just the beginning. Data science is a vast and ever-evolving field, and there is always more to learn. My hope is that this book will serve as a foundation, sparking your curiosity and motivating you to delve deeper into the world of data science.

Thank you for joining me on this adventure. I am excited to share my knowledge and experiences with you, and I look forward to seeing the incredible things you will achieve with the power of data. Let's dive in and explore the boundless possibilities that data science has to offer!

With warm regards,
Nitin.

MODULE 1

Introduction to Data Science

Unveiling the Mysteries of Data: A Journey into the World of Possibilities

Welcome, curious minds, to the thrilling realm of data science! Prepare to embark on an exhilarating journey through the vast landscapes of data, where mysteries await unraveling and insights lie hidden beneath the surface. In this module, we'll dive headfirst into the captivating world of data science, uncovering its mysteries, marvels, and the countless ways it shapes our modern existence.

What is Data Science?

Ah, the age-old question: What on earth is data science, anyway? Well, imagine yourself as a modern-day alchemist, wielding not a philosopher's stone, but a powerful set of tools and techniques to transmute raw data into pure knowledge gold. Data science, my friends, is the magical art of extracting meaning from chaos, turning bits and bytes into actionable insights.

Data science is the dynamic field that explores the art of deciphering complex data sets to extract valuable insights and knowledge. Data scientists dive deep into oceans of information, uncovering patterns, trends, and correlations that may be hidden to the untrained eye. At its core, data science combines elements of statistics, computer science, and domain expertise to make sense of the vast amounts of data generated in today's digital world. It's a blend of creativity and technical skill, where practitioners use algorithms, machine learning, and data visualization to transform raw data into actionable intelligence.

In essence, data science is the art of turning data into insights, driving innovation, informing decision-making, and unlocking new possibilities across diverse fields. It's about harnessing the power of data to solve problems, answer questions, and ultimately, make the world a better place.

The Astonishing Power of Data

Imagine this: you're standing on the bustling streets of a city, surrounded by a sea of people moving in every direction. Each person has a story to tell, a unique journey that has brought them to this very moment. Now, what if I told you that every step they take, every word they speak, every purchase they make, is being recorded? That's right – we live in a world where data is constantly being generated, captured, and analyzed at an unprecedented scale.

But what exactly is data, and why should we care? Well, dear reader, that's precisely what we're here to explore in this exhilarating journey into the realm of data science. Buckle up and get ready to uncover the mysteries of data, as we embark on an adventure filled with intrigue, excitement, and boundless possibilities!

The Data Revolution Begins

In the not-so-distant past, the term "data" might have conjured up images of boring spreadsheets and endless rows of numbers. But oh, how times have changed! Today, data is the lifeblood of our digital age, fueling everything from cutting-edge technologies to everyday conveniences.

Let's take a moment to consider a real-life example: the mighty smartphone in your pocket. From the moment you wake up to the sound of its alarm, to the late-night chats with friends before bed, your smartphone is constantly collecting data about your habits, preferences, and interactions. Every app you use, every website you visit, leaves behind a trail of digital breadcrumbs – valuable insights waiting to be discovered.

The Rise of Data Science Superheroes

Now, you might be wondering: who are the masterminds behind the scenes, unraveling the secrets hidden within the vast expanse of data? Enter the heroes of our story – the data scientists! With their unparalleled skills in mathematics, statistics, and computer science, data scientists possess the superhuman ability to sift through mountains of data, extracting nuggets of wisdom and knowledge.

But fear not, dear reader, for you too can join the ranks of these modern-day superheroes! Whether you're a coding prodigy or a curious novice, the world of data science welcomes all who dare to dream big and think outside the box.

Everyday Miracles: The Impact of Data Science

But enough talk – let's dive into the real magic of data science: its transformative power to shape the world around us. Take, for instance, the field of healthcare. Thanks to data-driven innovations, doctors can now diagnose diseases with greater accuracy, predict patient outcomes, and even personalize treatment plans based on individual genetic profiles.

Or consider the realm of finance, where data science is revolutionizing the way we manage money. From algorithmic trading to fraud detection, data-driven insights are reshaping the way businesses operate and consumers interact with their finances.

UNIT 1

Understanding the importance of data science in everyday life

The Power of Data in Everyday Life

Let's start by taking a stroll down memory lane to a time before smartphones, social media, and streaming services. Back then, data might have seemed like a distant concept – something reserved for scientists in white lab coats or number-crunching accountants. But oh, how times have changed!

In today's digital age, data is everywhere we look, from the moment we wake up to the sound of our alarm clocks, to the late-night scrolling sessions before bed. Each interaction we have with our devices leaves behind a digital footprint – a trail of breadcrumbs that tells the story of who we are, what we like, and where we're going.

Data Science in Action: A Closer Look

But enough talk – let's dive into some real-life examples of data science applications that are shaping the world as we know it. Take, for instance, the field of healthcare. Thanks to advances in data science, doctors and researchers can now analyze vast amounts of patient data to diagnose diseases, predict treatment outcomes, and even identify potential epidemics before they spread.

Imagine a world where doctors can pinpoint the exact genetic mutations that cause cancer, allowing them to tailor treatments to each patient's unique genetic makeup. Or consider the power of predictive analytics in healthcare, where machine learning algorithms can forecast patient readmissions or identify individuals at high risk of developing chronic conditions.

Data Science in Business: Driving Innovation and Growth

But data science isn't just revolutionizing healthcare – it's also transforming the way businesses operate and compete in today's digital marketplace. From retail giants like Amazon to tech titans like Google, companies of all shapes and sizes are harnessing the power of data to drive innovation, improve efficiency, and stay ahead of the competition.

Take, for example, the world of e-commerce. By analyzing customer browsing habits, purchase histories, and demographic data, online retailers can personalize product recommendations, optimize pricing strategies, and even predict future trends. And let's not forget about the role of data science in marketing, where targeted advertising and customer segmentation are reshaping the way businesses engage with consumers.

Data Science in the Wild: From Smart Cities to Environmental Conservation

But wait – there's more! Data science isn't just confined to the realms of healthcare and business – it's also making a big impact in areas like urban planning, environmental conservation, and beyond. Consider the concept of smart cities, where sensors and IoT devices collect real-time data on everything from traffic patterns to air quality, allowing city planners to optimize infrastructure and improve quality of life for residents.

Or think about the role of data science in environmental conservation, where satellite imagery, GIS mapping, and machine learning algorithms are helping scientists track deforestation, monitor wildlife populations, and combat climate change. By analyzing petabytes of data from sources around the globe, researchers can gain valuable insights into the health of our planet and take action to protect it for future generations.

The Future of Data Science: A World of Endless Possibilities

As we come to the end of our exploration into the world of data science applications, let us pause to reflect on the incredible journey we've undertaken. From healthcare to business, from smart cities to environmental conservation, data science has truly become the driving force behind some of the most significant advancements and innovations of our time.

But this is only the beginning – the tip of the iceberg, if you will. As technology continues to evolve and data volumes continue to grow, the possibilities for data science are truly endless. So, I invite you to join me as we embark on this thrilling adventure into the unknown, armed with nothing but our curiosity, our creativity, and our insatiable thirst for knowledge.

UNIT 2

Introduction to Basic Data Concepts and Terminology

The ABCs of Data: Understanding the Building Blocks

Welcome, dear reader, to the fascinating world of data – a world where every bit and byte holds the key to unlocking untold treasures of knowledge and insight. But before we dive headfirst into the depths of data science, let's take a moment to lay the groundwork and familiarize ourselves with some basic data concepts and terminology.

What is Data, Anyway?

At its core, data is simply a collection of facts, figures, or observations that have been recorded and stored for future reference. But don't let its simplicity fool you – data comes in many shapes and sizes, each with its own unique characteristics and properties.

For example, consider the humble spreadsheet – a staple tool in the arsenal of data scientists everywhere. In a spreadsheet, data is typically organized into rows and columns, with each row representing a single observation or "record," and each column representing a different "variable" or piece of information.

The Language of Data: Key Terminology to Know

As we journey deeper into the world of data, it's essential to familiarize ourselves with some key terminology that will serve as our guide along the way. Here are a few terms you'll want to commit to memory:

Variable: A variable is a characteristic or attribute that can take on different values. For example, in a dataset of student grades, variables might include "test scores," "homework grades," and "attendance records."

Observation: An observation is a single instance or data point within a dataset. Each row in a spreadsheet represents a single observation, while each column represents a different variable.

Dataset: A dataset is a collection of related data points or observations. Datasets can come in many forms, from simple spreadsheets to complex databases containing millions of records.

Descriptive Statistics: Descriptive statistics are numerical summaries that describe the main features of a dataset. Common descriptive statistics include measures of central tendency (e.g., mean, median, mode) and measures of dispersion (e.g., standard deviation, range).

Inferential Statistics: Inferential statistics are techniques used to draw conclusions or make predictions about a population based on a sample of data. These techniques include hypothesis testing, regression analysis, and confidence intervals.

From Raw Data to Insights: The Data Analysis Process

Now that we've covered the basics, let's talk about how we can turn raw data into meaningful insights and discoveries. This process, known as data analysis, typically involves several key steps:

Data Collection: The first step in the data analysis process is collecting the data itself. This might involve gathering data from existing sources, such as databases or websites, or collecting new data through surveys, experiments, or observations.

Data Cleaning: Once we have our data, the next step is to clean it – that is, to identify and correct any errors, inconsistencies, or missing values. This might involve removing duplicate entries, filling in missing data, or standardizing formats.

Exploratory Data Analysis (EDA): With our data cleaned and ready to go, it's time to explore! Exploratory data analysis involves visually inspecting the data, looking for patterns, trends, or anomalies that might warrant further investigation. This might involve creating histograms, scatter plots, or box plots to visualize the distribution of the data.

Statistical Analysis: Once we've explored our data, we can move on to more formal statistical analysis techniques. This might involve calculating descriptive statistics to summarize the main features of the data, or performing inferential statistics to make predictions or draw conclusions about a population.

Putting It All Together: A Hands-On Exercise

To bring our exploration of basic data concepts to life, let's dive into a hands-on exercise together. Imagine we have a dataset containing information about the heights and weights of a group of students. Using the concepts we've learned, we could:

Calculate the mean and median height and weight of the students.

Create a scatter plot to visualize the relationship between height and weight.

Perform a hypothesis test to determine if there is a significant difference in height between male and female students.

Conclusion

As we come to the end of our exploration into the realm of basic data concepts and terminology, let us pause to reflect on all that we've learned. From the humble spreadsheet to the complexities of statistical analysis, we've covered a lot of ground in our journey together.

But remember, dear reader, this is only the beginning. The world of data science is vast and ever-evolving, with new discoveries waiting to be made around every corner. So, take what you've learned here today and let it be the foundation upon which you build your own data-driven adventures.

The future is yours to explore – so go forth, armed with knowledge, curiosity, and a thirst for discovery. The world of data awaits!

MODULE 2
Data Collection and Analysis

UNIT 1

Learning methods of data collection

The Quest for the Golden Data

Imagine embarking on an adventurous treasure hunt. You've got your map, your compass, and a sense of excitement bubbling within you. Now, imagine that instead of gold coins and ancient relics, the treasure you're hunting for is data. Yes, data – those nuggets of information that hold the power to reveal secrets, solve mysteries, and unlock opportunities. In this chapter, we'll equip you with the tools and knowledge needed to collect and analyze this valuable treasure. So, grab your explorer's hat, and let's begin our quest for the golden data!

The Data Hunter's Toolkit

Before we set out on our adventure, it's crucial to understand that data doesn't just fall into our laps. We need to actively collect it, much like a detective gathering clues. There are various methods of data collection, each suited to different types of investigations. Let's delve into the main methods:

Surveys and Questionnaires: The People's Voice

Surveys and questionnaires are like the friendly villagers in our treasure hunt, each offering pieces of the map. By asking people a series of questions, we can gather valuable information about their opinions, behaviors, and preferences. For example, a company might use a survey to understand customer satisfaction, while a researcher might use it to gather data on public health trends.

Example: Think about the last time you filled out a feedback form after dining at a restaurant. Your responses helped the restaurant understand what you liked or didn't like, enabling them to improve their service.

Interviews: The Storytellers

Interviews are akin to sitting by a campfire, listening to the tales of seasoned adventurers. They involve one-on-one conversations where detailed information is gathered through direct interaction. This method is particularly useful for collecting qualitative data – rich, descriptive insights that go beyond mere numbers.

Example: Imagine a journalist interviewing an athlete about their journey to the Olympics. The interview provides in-depth insights into the athlete's experiences, challenges, and triumphs.

Observations: The Silent Watchers

Sometimes, the best way to gather data is by quietly observing the world around us. Observational methods involve watching and recording behaviors and events as they occur naturally. This can be particularly useful in fields like anthropology, psychology, and market research.

Example: A wildlife biologist observing the behavior of animals in their natural habitat collects valuable data without interfering with their environment.

Experiments: The Controlled Environments

In our quest for data, we might sometimes create controlled environments to test specific hypotheses. Experiments involve manipulating variables to observe their effects, allowing us to draw conclusions about cause and effect relationships.

Example: A scientist conducting a laboratory experiment to test the efficacy of a new drug collects data on its impact on health outcomes.

Existing Data: The Ancient Scrolls

Not all data needs to be collected from scratch. Sometimes, the treasure we seek is already hidden in plain sight within existing records, databases, and archives. Secondary data analysis involves using data that has already been collected for other purposes.

Example: A historian analyzing census records to study demographic changes over time relies on existing data to uncover patterns and trends.

UNIT 2

Introduction to Data Types and Data Structures

With our toolkit in hand, it's time to delve deeper into the types of data we might encounter on our quest. Understanding the different types of data and how they can be structured is essential for effective analysis and interpretation.

Data Types: The Diverse Treasures

Qualitative Data: The Rich Narratives

Qualitative data, often referred to as categorical data, consists of descriptive information that can't be easily quantified. It's like the vibrant stories and legends passed down through generations – rich in detail and context.

Example: Customer reviews of a product, interview transcripts, and field notes from observations all constitute qualitative data.

Quantitative Data: The Numerical Gems

Quantitative data, on the other hand, is numerical in nature and can be measured and analyzed using statistical methods. It's like the precise coordinates on a treasure map, providing clear and specific information.

Example: The number of steps you've taken in a day, your test scores, and the revenue generated by a company are all examples of quantitative data.

The Great Divide: Discrete vs. Continuous Data

Quantitative data can be further divided into discrete and continuous types, each with its own unique characteristics:

Discrete Data: The Countable Coins

Discrete data consists of countable values that can't be subdivided meaningfully. It's like counting the number of gold coins in your treasure chest – you can have 10 coins or 15 coins, but not 10.5 coins.

Example: The number of students in a classroom, the number of cars in a parking lot, and the number of books on a shelf are all examples of discrete data.

Continuous Data: The Fluid Streams

Continuous data, on the other hand, can take on any value within a given range. It's like the flowing streams of a river, where the water can be measured at any point along its course.

Example: The height of students, the time it takes to complete a race and the temperature throughout the day are all examples of continuous data.

Data Structures: Organizing the Treasure Trove

Now that we've explored the different types of data, let's talk about how we can organize and structure this data for analysis. Think of data structures as the treasure chests and vaults that keep our data organized and accessible.

Arrays: The Ordered Lists

Arrays are like neat rows of treasure chests, each containing a specific item. An array is a collection of elements (values or variables) that are indexed by a single variable. Arrays can be one-dimensional or multi-dimensional, depending on the complexity of the data.

Example: A list of test scores [85, 90, 78, 92] is an example of a one-dimensional array. A table of student grades with subjects and scores is an example of a two-dimensional array.

Lists: The Flexible Collections

Lists are similar to arrays but offer more flexibility. They can store elements of different types and can be easily modified by adding or removing elements. Lists are like the versatile bags of a treasure hunter, capable of holding a variety of items.

Example: A shopping list that includes items like "apples," "bananas," and "milk" is an example of a list. The list can be easily updated as needed.

Dictionaries: The Key-Value Pairs

Dictionaries, also known as associative arrays or hash maps, are collections of key-value pairs. They are like the treasure maps with markers indicating the locations of hidden treasures. Each key is unique and is used to retrieve the corresponding value.

Example: A dictionary of student grades might look like {"Alice": 85, "Bob": 90, "Charlie": 78}. Each student's name is a key, and their grade is the corresponding value.

Data Frames: The Tabular Treasures

Data frames are tabular data structures that allow us to store and manipulate data in a spreadsheet-like format. They are essential tools for data analysis, providing a structured way to organize and analyze complex datasets.

Example: A data frame containing information about students might have columns for "Name," "Age," "Grade," and "Attendance." Each row represents a different student, and each column represents a different variable.

Hands-On Exercise: Creating Your Own Data Structures

To solidify our understanding of data structures, let's embark on a hands-on exercise. Imagine we're collecting data on a group of treasure hunters, including their names, ages, and the number of treasures they've found. Here's how we might organize this data using different structures:

Array: We could create an array of ages, such as [25, 32, 28, 35].

List: We could create a list of names, such as ["Alice," "Bob," "Charlie," "David"].

Dictionary: We could create a dictionary of treasures found, such as {"Alice": 5, "Bob": 3, "Charlie": 8, "David": 2}.

Data Frame: We could create a data frame to store all the information together:

Name	Age	Treasures Found
Alice	25	5
Bob	32	3
Charlie	28	8
David	35	2

By organizing our data in these structures, we make it easier to analyze and draw meaningful insights from it.

MODULE 3
Introduction to Programming

UNIT 1

Introduction to Programming: Basic concepts of programming using Python

Welcome, young adventurers, to the enchanting world of programming! Imagine yourself as a wizard wielding a powerful wand called Python, ready to conjure spells that bring your wildest ideas to life. In this chapter, we'll embark on a thrilling journey to unlock the secrets of programming and harness its boundless creativity. So grab your spellbook, don your wizard hat, and let's dive into the mystical realm of coding!

Please note that I have written an ebook and a paperback edition on Python programming simplified. It is to make it easy for you to understand the Python concepts and fundamentals and it is available on Amazon. You may want to search it on your amazon app/website. Here is a picture to make it easy for you:

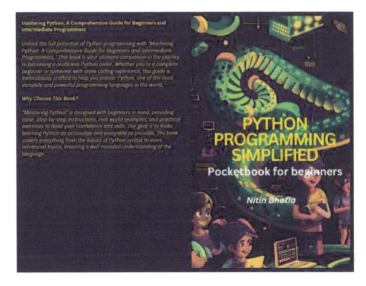

The Magical Language of Computers

Before we delve into the mystical art of programming, let's unravel the mystery of how computers understand our commands. Imagine you're chatting with a magical creature, say a dragon named Byte. Now, Byte may be wise and mighty, but it only speaks one language – the language of 0s and 1s, also known as binary code. Try telling Byte to breathe fire with just 0s and 1s – quite the tongue twister, isn't it?

But fear not, for we have a magical translator called a programming language! Just like wizards casting spells, programmers use these languages to communicate with computers in a way they understand. And one of the most enchanting languages in our arsenal is Python – a friendly and versatile tongue loved by wizards of all ages.

Unleashing Python's Spellbinding Powers

Example 1: Hello, World!

Every wizard's journey begins with a humble incantation, and in the world of programming, that spell is "Hello, World!" Let's cast this spell together and make our mark on the digital realm:

```python
print("Hello, World!")
```

Behold the magic! With just a few lines of Python code, we've summoned a message that echoes across the digital ether. Isn't it marvelous how a few keystrokes can wield such power?

Example 2: Potion Brewing with Variables

In our wizarding adventures, we often need to store magical ingredients for later use. That's where variables come in handy – they're like tiny vials that hold our potions. Let's brew a simple potion to dazzle our senses:

```python
ingredient1 = "unicorn tears"
ingredient2 = "dragon scales"
potion = ingredient1 + " and " + ingredient2
print("Behold, a potion of", potion)
```

By combining our magical ingredients, we've concocted a potion worthy of the most daring adventurers. With variables, the possibilities are as endless as the stars in the night sky!

Example 3: Enchanting Loops

What's a wizard without a bit of repetition? Loops are our trusty companions for casting spells multiple times without breaking a sweat. Let's summon a flock of enchanted birds with a loop:

```
for bird in range(5):
    print("Flap your wings, little birdie!")
```

Look at them go! With just a few lines of code, we've brought forth a chorus of fluttering wings. Loops are like magical echoes that reverberate through the digital forest.

The Quest Continues...

As our journey through the enchanted realm of Python comes to a close, remember that this is just the beginning of your adventures in programming. There are countless spells yet to be discovered, mysteries waiting to be unraveled, and dragons waiting to be tamed. So keep your wand at the ready, your mind sharp, and let the magic of code guide you on your quest!

UNIT 2

Introduction to coding environments like Jupyter Notebooks

Now that we've mastered the basics of Python spells, it's time to venture into the enchanted realms of coding environments and unleash our newfound powers on the mystical art of data manipulation. Prepare to be amazed as we embark on this thrilling quest together!

The Magic of Coding Environments

Before we dive into our spellcasting adventures, let's first uncover the secret chambers where wizards like us weave their digital magic. Enter the world of coding environments – mystical realms where spells come to life and dreams take flight.

What are Coding Environments?

Imagine a wizard's workshop, filled with magical tools and artifacts, where every incantation and potion recipe springs to life. Coding environments are just like that – they're special places where wizards (or programmers, in our case) write and execute their spells (code) with ease.

One such enchanting abode is called Jupyter Notebooks – a magical parchment where wizards can write Python spells, weave together text and code, and even conjure visual enchantments like charts and graphs.

Introducing Jupyter Notebooks

Jupyter Notebooks are like enchanted scrolls that blend prose and code seamlessly, allowing wizards to document their adventures, experiment with spells, and share their magical creations with fellow enchanters.

How to Summon Jupyter Notebooks

To embark on your own Jupyter journey, you'll need to summon it from the depths of the digital realm. Fear not, for I shall guide you through the summoning ritual step by step:

1. **Open Your Browser**: Navigate to your favorite browser – be it Chrome, Firefox, or Safari. The digital gates await your command!
2. **Invoke the Spell**: Type "Jupyter Notebook" into your browser's search bar and press Enter. The mystical portal to Jupyter shall appear before your very eyes.
3. **Cast the Incantation**: Click on the sacred link that beckons you to the official Jupyter website. Here, you'll find the sacred scrolls you seek.
4. **Channel Your Magic**: Follow the instructions to download and install Jupyter Notebook on your magical device. With a flick of your wand (or a click of your mouse), the installation process shall commence.
5. **Open the Portal**: Once installed, summon Jupyter Notebook from your digital arsenal. A new tab shall open in your browser, revealing the gateway to the mystical world of coding.

The Magic Within: Writing Simple Scripts

Now that we've conjured our Jupyter Notebook and stepped into the realm of coding, it's time to wield our Python spells with finesse. Let's begin our journey by mastering the art of writing simple scripts to manipulate and analyze data – a skill prized by wizards and enchanters alike.

Example 1: Summoning Data from the Depths

Every wizard knows that knowledge is power, and in the realm of coding, data is our most potent weapon. Let's cast a spell to summon a dataset from the depths of the digital sea:

```python
import pandas as pd

# Summon the Dataset
url = 'https://raw.githubusercontent.com/datasciencedojo/datasets/master/titanic.csv'
data = pd.read_csv(url)

# Display the First Few Rows
data.head()
```

Behold! With just a few lines of Python code, we've summoned the Titanic dataset – a trove of knowledge waiting to be explored. Pandas, our trusty familiar, has helped us bring this data to life with ease.

Example 2: Unveiling the Secrets Within

Now that we've summoned our dataset, let's peer into its depths and uncover its hidden secrets. With a simple spell, we can reveal the first few rows of our dataset and glimpse the wonders it holds:

```python
# Display the First Few Rows
data.head()
```

Marvelous, isn't it? In just a heartbeat, we've unveiled the secrets of the Titanic dataset – its passengers, their fates, and the stories that lie buried within.

Example 3: Casting Spells of Transformation

But wait – our journey doesn't end here! With Python by our side, we can transform our dataset, bend it to our will, and unleash its true potential. Let's cast a spell to filter the data and uncover the fate of the brave souls aboard the Titanic:

```
# Filter the Data: Survivors
survivors = data[data['Survived'] == 1]

# Display the First Few Rows of Survivors
survivors.head()
```

By filtering the data, we've revealed the brave souls who survived the Titanic's fateful voyage. With each line of code, we gain new insights and unravel the mysteries of the past.

UNIT 3

Writing Simple Scripts to Manipulate and Analyze Data

Now that we've dipped our toes into the mystical waters of coding environments and summoned the power of Python, it's time to dive deeper. Today, we'll explore how to write simple yet powerful scripts to manipulate and analyze data. Prepare to wield your wand (keyboard) as we uncover more secrets hidden within our datasets.

The Art of Data Manipulation

In the wizarding world of programming, data manipulation is akin to shaping raw materials into wondrous artifacts. With Python and its magical libraries, we can mold our data to fit our needs and uncover hidden patterns. Let's embark on this adventure with some hands-on examples.

Example 1: Cleaning the Data

Every wizard knows that a clean workspace is crucial for casting successful spells. Similarly, clean data is essential for accurate analysis. Let's cast a spell to cleanse our dataset of any impurities:

Problem: We have a dataset that contains missing values and unnecessary columns. How can we clean this data to make it ready for analysis?

Dataset: Here's a small sample of the Titanic dataset:

PassengerId	Name	Pclass	Age	Cabin	Ticket	Fare	Embarked
1	Braund, Mr. Owen Harris	3	22	None	A/5 21171	7.25	S
2	Cumings, Mrs. John Bradley (Florence Briggs)	1	38	C85	PC 17599	71.2833	C
3	Heikkinen, Miss. Laina	3	26	None	STON/O2. 3101282	7.925	S
4	Futrelle, Mrs. Jacques Heath (Lily May Peel)	1	35	C123	113803	53.1	S
5	Allen, Mr. William Henry	3	None	None	373450	8.05	None

Solution: We will write a Python script to remove unnecessary columns and fill in the missing values.

Script:

```python
# Remove Columns Not Needed
cleaned_data = data.drop(['Cabin', 'Ticket'], axis=1)

# Fill Missing Values
cleaned_data['Age'].fillna(cleaned_data['Age'].median(), inplace=True)
cleaned_data['Embarked'].fillna(cleaned_data['Embarked'].mode()[0], inplace=True)

# Display the First Few Rows of Cleaned Data
cleaned_data.head()
```

Answer:

By running the script, we remove the 'Cabin' and 'Ticket' columns from our dataset as they are not needed for our analysis. We also fill in missing values in the 'Age' column with the median age and the 'Embarked' column with the most common value. Here's a glimpse of our cleaned data:

PassengerId	Name	Pclass	Age	Fare	Embarked
1	Braund, Mr. Owen Harris	3	22	7.25	S
2	Cumings, Mrs. John Bradley (Florence Briggs)	1	38	71.28	C
3	Heikkinen, Miss. Laina	3	26	7.925	S
4	Futrelle, Mrs. Jacques Heath (Lily May Peel)	1	35	53.1	S
5	Allen, Mr. William Henry	3	30	8.05	S

Example 2: Summoning Descriptive Statistics

Problem: How can we get a quick summary of our dataset to understand its structure and key statistics?

Dataset: We will use the cleaned Titanic dataset from Example 1.

Solution: We will use Python to calculate descriptive statistics for our dataset.

Script:

```python
# Summon Descriptive Statistics
description = cleaned_data.describe()

# Display Descriptive Statistics
description
```

Answer:

Running this script provides a summary of our dataset, including the count, mean, standard deviation, minimum, and maximum values for each numerical column. This summary helps us understand the overall structure and tendencies of our data:

	PassengerId	Pclass	Age	Fare
count	5	5	5	5
mean	3	2.2	30.2	29.92
std	1.58	1.095	6.686	26.99
min	1	1	22	7.25
25%	2	1	26	7.925
50%	3	3	30	8.05
75%	4	3	35	53.1
max	5	3	38	71.28

MODULE 4

Data Visualization

UNIT 1

Understanding the importance of data visualization

The Power of Visualization

Imagine you're in a room full of people, and you're asked to describe your day. Instead of talking about your day in a typical way, you decide to make it a bit more interesting. You pull out a whiteboard and start drawing pictures. You draw the sun shining in the morning, a bus taking you to school, a book you read, and a soccer ball representing your game after school. Suddenly, everyone in the room is paying attention. They can see your day, and it's much easier to understand.

That's the magic of data visualization! Just like drawing pictures of your day, data visualization helps us turn complex data into easy-to-understand visuals. Instead of getting lost in a sea of numbers and text, we use charts, graphs, and images to tell a story.

Why Visualization Matters

Let's start with a real-life example. Imagine you're a detective, and you've collected tons of clues and evidence. Now, you have to solve the mystery. If you just look at a list of clues, it might be confusing. But what if you had a big board where you could pin photos, connect them with strings, and highlight important details? Suddenly, the mystery becomes much clearer.

Data visualization is like that detective board. It helps us make sense of data by showing patterns, trends, and outliers. It turns data into something visual, something we can see and understand at a glance.

Example: Social Media Usage

Consider how much time teenagers spend on different social media platforms. If you had a table full of numbers showing hours spent on each platform by different age groups, it might be a bit overwhelming. But what if you had a colorful pie chart?

Table of Social Media Usage:

Platform	Hours per Week
Instagram	10
Snapchat	8
TikTok	12
Facebook	4
Twitter	6

Now, let's visualize this data with a pie chart:

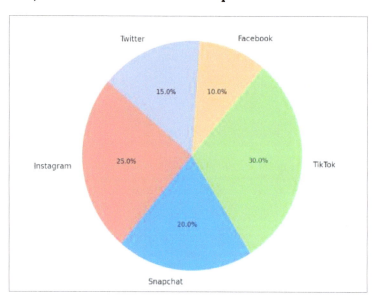

This chart shows the proportion of hours spent on different social media platforms per week. You can see that TikTok takes up the largest slice, followed by Instagram and Snapchat. Facebook and Twitter have smaller slices, indicating less usage.

Types of Data Visualizations

There are many different types of data visualizations, each suited for different kinds of data and purposes. Let's explore some of the most common ones.

1. Bar Charts

Bar charts are great for comparing different groups. They use bars to show the values of each group.

Example: Favorite School Subjects

Imagine we surveyed 100 students about their favorite subjects. Here are the results:

Subject	Number of Students
Math	30
Science	25
History	20
English	15
Art	10

Now, let's create a bar chart to visualize this data:

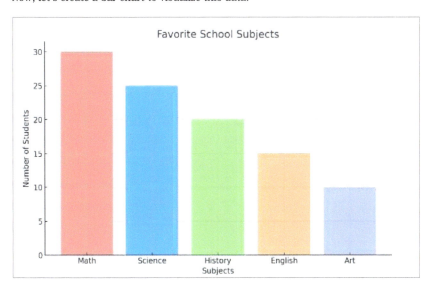

From the bar chart, it's clear that Math is the most popular subject, followed by Science and History.

2. Line Charts

Line charts are perfect for showing trends over time. They use lines to connect data points, making it easy to see how something changes.

Example: Temperature Changes

Imagine we recorded the temperature every hour for a day. Here are the temperatures:

Hour	Temperature (°C)
1	15
2	14
3	13
4	12
5	12
6	13
7	15
8	18
9	20
10	22
11	24
12	25
13	26
14	27
15	28
16	27
17	25
18	23
19	21
20	19
21	17
22	16
23	15
24	14

Let's create a line chart to visualize this data:

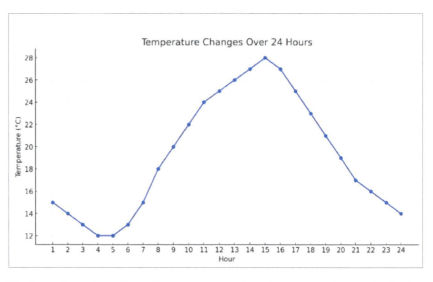

The line chart shows how the temperature rises in the morning, peaks in the afternoon, and falls in the evening.

3. Scatter Plots

Scatter plots are used to show the relationship between two variables. They use dots to represent data points.

Example: Height and Shoe Size

Imagine we recorded the height and shoe size of 10 students:

Student	Height (cm)	Shoe Size
A	150	38
B	155	39
C	160	40
D	165	41
E	170	42
F	175	43
G	180	44
H	185	45
I	190	46
J	195	47

Let's create a scatter plot to visualize this data:

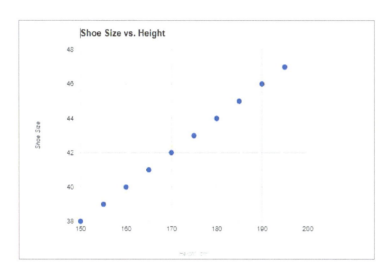

The scatter plot shows that as height increases, shoe size also tends to increase.

The Importance of Clear Visuals

Creating clear and accurate visualizations is crucial. A good visualization should be easy to understand and convey the right message.

Data visualization is a powerful tool that turns complex data into understandable and engaging visuals. Whether you're analyzing social media usage, tracking temperatures, or studying the relationship between height and shoe size, visualizations make it easier to see patterns and make decisions.

By learning how to create and interpret various types of charts and graphs, you'll be able to present your data in a way that tells a clear and compelling story. So grab your markers, open your favorite coding environment, and start transforming data into amazing visuals!

Unit 2

Introduction to Visualization Libraries like Matplotlib and Seaborn

Introduction: The Magic of Visualization

Hey there, budding data scientists! Have you ever heard the saying, "A picture is worth a thousand words?" Well, in the world of data science, it's absolutely true! Imagine trying to explain how a roller coaster's speed changes over time using just numbers. Boring, right? But if you draw a graph, suddenly it becomes an exciting story of ups and downs! Today, we're diving into the colorful world of data visualization using two magical tools: Matplotlib and Seaborn. Ready? Let's paint some data!

What is a Terminal?

Before we start, let's talk about the "terminal." Think of it as a magic portal to the world of commands and coding. It's a text-based interface where you can type commands to tell your computer what to do. On Windows, it's called the Command Prompt, and on macOS and Linux, it's just called Terminal. Don't worry; it's not as scary as it sounds!

How to Open the Command Line Prompt:

For Windows:

Press the Windows Key on your keyboard.

Type cmd and hit Enter. You should see a black window with a blinking cursor. That's the Command Prompt!

For macOS:

1. Press Cmd + Space to open Spotlight Search.
2. Type Terminal and hit Enter. A window with a white background and some text should appear. That's your Terminal!

For Linux:

1. Press Ctrl + Alt + T. A terminal window should pop up.

Installing Matplotlib and Seaborn

To create stunning visualizations, we need to install two Python libraries: Matplotlib and Seaborn. These are like our paintbrushes and canvas. Here's how to install them using the terminal:

1. Open your terminal or command prompt.
2. Type the following command and press Enter:

```
C:\>python
```

If Python is not installed on your computer it will install it.if it is, then input the following command

Open the command prompt again and

```
pip install matplotlib seaborn
```

This command tells your computer to fetch and install Matplotlib and Seaborn from the internet. You'll see some text flying by as it installs. Once it's done, you're ready to start creating beautiful charts!

What is Matplotlib?

Matplotlib is like your basic but versatile set of colored pencils. You can draw almost anything with it, from simple line charts to complex scatter plots. It's the go-to tool for most data scientists when they need to create quick and effective visualizations.

Getting Started with Matplotlib

Let's jump into some examples. Imagine we have some data about the number of ice creams sold in a week. Here's how we can visualize that using Matplotlib:

```python
import matplotlib.pyplot as plt

# Data
days = ['Monday', 'Tuesday', 'Wednesday', 'Thursday', 'Friday', 'Saturday', 'Sunday']
ice_creams_sold = [20, 25, 15, 30, 45, 50, 60]

# Create a bar chart
plt.figure(figsize=(10, 6))
plt.bar(days, ice_creams_sold, color='skyblue')
plt.xlabel('Days of the Week')
plt.ylabel('Number of Ice Creams Sold')
plt.title('Ice Cream Sales in a Week')
plt.show()
```

Explanation:

- We start by importing matplotlib.pyplot as plt.
- We define our data: days of the week and ice_creams_sold.
- We create a bar chart using the bar function.
- We add labels and a title to make the chart more informative.
- Finally, we use plt.show() to display the chart.

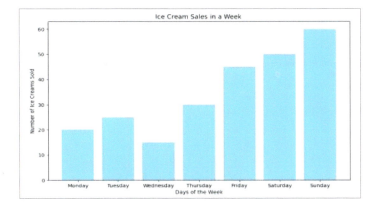

Example : Line Chart of Daily Temperatures

Let's say we recorded the temperature at noon every day for a week. Here's how we can visualize that data:

```python
import matplotlib.pyplot as plt

# Data
days = ['Monday', 'Tuesday', 'Wednesday', 'Thursday', 'Friday', 'Saturday', 'Sunday']
temperatures = [22, 24, 19, 23, 25, 28, 26]

# Create a line chart
plt.figure(figsize=(10, 6))
plt.plot(days, temperatures, marker='o', linestyle='-', color='tomato')
plt.xlabel('Days of the Week')
plt.ylabel('Temperature (°C)')
plt.title('Daily Temperatures at Noon')
plt.grid(True)
plt.show()
```

Explanation:

- We define our days and temperatures.
- We create a line chart using the plot function, with markers for each data point and a tomato red line.
- We add labels, a title, and a grid for better readability.
- Finally, we display the chart.

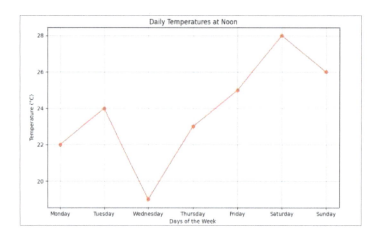

What is Seaborn?

Seaborn is like an advanced set of art supplies. It's built on top of Matplotlib and provides beautiful and informative statistical graphics. It makes it easy to create more complex visualizations with less code.

Getting Started with Seaborn

Now, let's dive into Seaborn. Suppose we have data about the scores of students in different subjects. Here's how we can create a box plot to visualize that:

```python
import seaborn as sns
import matplotlib.pyplot as plt

# Data
data = {
    'Subjects': ['Math', 'Science', 'History', 'English', 'Art'] * 10,
    'Scores': [88, 92, 75, 85, 90, 78, 85, 80, 83, 76, 85, 87, 77, 88, 93, 91, 89, 84,
               79, 82, 80, 81, 83, 86, 84, 87, 88, 89, 92, 90, 85, 84, 86, 88, 81, 80,
}

# Create a box plot
plt.figure(figsize=(10, 6))
sns.boxplot(x='Subjects', y='Scores', data=data, palette='Set2')
plt.xlabel('Subjects')
plt.ylabel('Scores')
plt.title('Distribution of Student Scores by Subject')
plt.show()
```

The code is:

```
import seaborn as sns
import matplotlib.pyplot as plt
# Data
data = {
    'Subjects': ['Math', 'Science', 'History', 'English', 'Art'] * 10,
    'Scores': [88, 92, 75, 85, 90, 78, 85, 80, 83, 76, 85, 87, 77, 88, 93, 91, 89, 84, 86, 78,
           79, 82, 80, 81, 83, 86, 84, 87, 88, 89, 92, 90, 85, 84, 86, 88, 81, 80, 85, 87, 77, 80,
83, 86, 90, 91, 82, 85, 89, 87]
}
# Create a box plot
plt.figure(figsize=(10, 6))
sns.boxplot(x='Subjects', y='Scores', data=data, palette='Set2')
plt.xlabel('Subjects')
plt.ylabel('Scores')
plt.title('Distribution of Student Scores by Subject')
plt.show()
```

Explanation:

- We import seaborn as sns and matplotlib.pyplot as plt.
- We create a dictionary data with our subjects and scores.
- We create a box plot using sns.boxplot.
- We add labels and a title.
- Finally, we display the plot.

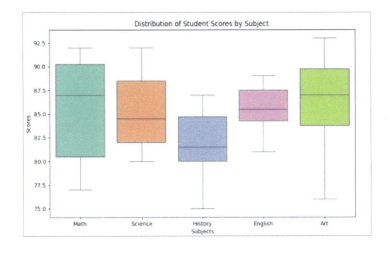

Example : Pair Plot of Iris Dataset

Seaborn comes with several built-in datasets, including the famous Iris dataset. Let's use it to create a pair plot:

```python
import seaborn as sns
import matplotlib.pyplot as plt

# Load the Iris dataset
iris = sns.load_dataset('iris')

# Create a pair plot
plt.figure(figsize=(12, 8))
sns.pairplot(iris, hue='species', palette='Set1')
plt.suptitle('Pair Plot of Iris Dataset', y=1.02)
plt.show()
```

Explanation:

- We load the Iris dataset using sns.load_dataset.
- We create a pair plot using sns.pairplot, coloring the points based on the species.
- We add a title to the plot.
- Finally, we display the plot.

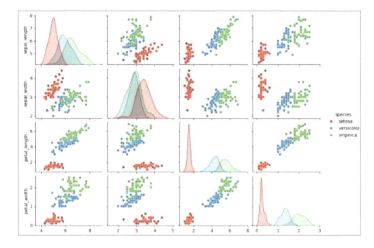

Bringing it All Together

Data visualization is a powerful tool that turns raw data into meaningful insights. Whether you're using Matplotlib for simple plots or Seaborn for more complex ones, the key is to make your visualizations clear and informative.

Remember, the goal of data visualization is to tell a story with your data. With the right tools and a bit of creativity, you can turn even the most boring data into a captivating visual story. So grab your paintbrushes—oops, I mean your Python code—and start visualizing!

MODULE 5

Machine Learning Basics

UNIT 1

Introduction to Machine Learning Concepts

Welcome aboard, young data scientists! Get ready to dive into the exciting world of machine learning, where computers learn from data and make decisions without being explicitly programmed. In this unit, we'll unravel the magic behind algorithms that power everything from movie recommendations to self-driving cars.

Section 1: What is Machine Learning?

Imagine teaching your dog a new trick. At first, you show them how to sit with a treat as a reward. After a few tries, they get it! Machine learning is similar but with computers instead of pets. It's a way for computers to learn from examples and experiences to improve over time.

Section 2: Types of Machine Learning

2.1 Supervised Learning

Think of this like teaching a kid with examples and answers. You show the computer lots of labeled data (inputs and correct outputs) to learn from. For instance, feeding it images of cats and dogs with labels to distinguish between them.

2.2 Unsupervised Learning

Here, the computer explores on its own, finding patterns and making sense of data without any labels. It's like sorting your LEGO bricks into piles without anyone telling you how.

2.3 Reinforcement Learning

Ever played a video game where you get better by trial and error? That's what reinforcement learning is like. The computer learns by taking actions and getting rewards or penalties. It's how robots learn to walk or play chess.

Section 3: Key Concepts in Machine Learning

3.1 Features and Labels

Features are the characteristics or attributes of our data. For example, in predicting the weather, features could include temperature, humidity, and wind speed. Labels are what we're trying to predict, like whether it will rain or not.

3.2 Training and Testing Data

Just like studying for a test, machine learning models need to practice. Training data teaches the model using examples, while testing data checks how well it learned by giving it new, unseen examples.

3.3 Algorithms: The Magic Recipe

Algorithms are like recipes telling computers how to learn from data. Each one has its strengths: some are good with pictures (like CNNs for recognizing faces), while others excel with words (like NLP models for understanding text).

Section 4: Real-World Applications

4.1 Self-Driving Cars

Imagine a car that drives itself using machine learning to recognize road signs, avoid obstacles, and even park on its own. It's like having a super-smart chauffeur!

4.2 Healthcare Predictions

Doctors can use machine learning to analyze medical records and predict diseases early. It's like having a crystal ball for your health!

4.3 Personalized Recommendations

Ever wonder how Netflix knows what movies you'll love? Machine learning! It analyzes your watching habits to suggest shows just for you.

Section 5: Ethics in Machine Learning

5.1 The Good and the Bad

While machine learning can do amazing things, it's essential to use it responsibly. Sometimes, biased data or decisions can lead to unfair outcomes. Understanding ethics helps us create fairer algorithms for everyone.

5.2 Your Role as a Data Scientist

As future data wizards, you'll have the power to shape how machines learn and make decisions. By thinking ethically and inclusively, you can create a brighter, fairer future with machine learning.

Section 6: Fun Facts and Trivia

- Did you know the first ever machine learning program was written in 1952? It played checkers and learned from its mistakes—just like you do!
- Machine learning isn't just for computers. Animals and even plants use similar techniques to adapt to their environments.

- The movie "Moneyball" shows how machine learning (in this case, statistical models) transformed baseball by picking players based on data, not just instinct.

Section 7: Let's Recap!

Congratulations! You've completed Unit 1 of Machine Learning Basics. Now, you're armed with the knowledge of how machines learn, different types of learning, and even how to start coding your own predictions. Stay tuned for Unit 2, where we'll dive deeper into building and fine-tuning your own machine learning models. Until then, keep exploring and experimenting—it's the heart of being a great data scientist!

Remember, the world of data science is vast and ever-growing. With your curiosity and creativity, there's no limit to what you can achieve. Get ready to change the world—one algorithm at a time!

UNIT 2

Understanding Supervised and Unsupervised Learning

Hey there, future data wizards! Welcome back to our journey through the fascinating world of machine learning. In Unit 1, we learned how computers learn from data. Now, let's dive deeper into two cool ways they do it: supervised and unsupervised learning. Don't worry—we'll keep it fun, simple, and totally jargon-free!

Section 1: Supervised Learning: Learning with Labels

Imagine you're teaching a robot to sort toys into different boxes. You show it each toy and tell it which box it belongs to. This process, where computers learn from labeled examples, is called **supervised learning**.

1.1 How Supervised Learning Works

In supervised learning, the computer learns by example. You give it pairs of inputs (like pictures of toys) and their correct labels (which box they should go into). The computer then figures out patterns to make predictions on new examples it hasn't seen before.

Example: Teaching a Robot Toys

Let's break it down step-by-step:

1. **Data Collection**: Gather pictures of different toys—like cars, dolls, and blocks—and label each picture with its correct name.

Toy Picture	Label
Car	Car
Doll	Doll
Block	Block

2. **Training the Model**: Now, teach the computer using these labeled pictures. It learns to recognize the patterns that make each toy unique.

3. **Making Predictions**: Once trained, the computer can predict which box a new toy belongs to, based on what it learned from the labeled examples.

1.2 Applications of Supervised Learning

- **Identifying Animals**: Teaching computers to recognize pictures of dogs, cats, and birds.
- **Predicting Grades**: Using past test scores to predict how well students might do on future tests.

- **Translating Languages**: Learning to translate English sentences into French or Spanish.

Section 2: Unsupervised Learning: Exploring on Its Own

Now, imagine the robot has a bunch of toys but no labels. It needs to figure out how to group them based on their similarities. This is called **unsupervised learning**.

2.1 How Unsupervised Learning Works

In unsupervised learning, the computer explores the data on its own. It looks for patterns or groups without any help from labels. It's like finding friends who like the same games as you, even if you didn't know them before!

Example: Sorting Toys Without Labels

Let's see how the robot can do this:

1. **Data Exploration**: Show the robot all the toys without telling it which box they go into. Let it explore and group toys that look similar.
2. **Finding Patterns**: The robot might notice that cars and trucks look similar because they both have wheels and are meant for driving around.
3. **Grouping Toys**: After exploring, the robot might put all the cars in one group and all the dolls in another, based on how they look and what they're used for.

2.2 Applications of Unsupervised Learning

- **Customer Segmentation**: Grouping customers based on their shopping habits.
- **Discovering Topics**: Sorting news articles into categories like sports, politics, and entertainment.
- **Recommendation Systems**: Suggesting new books or games based on what you've liked before.

Section 3: Key Differences Between Supervised and Unsupervised Learning

Let's compare what we've learned:

- **Goal**: Supervised learning predicts answers using labeled examples, while unsupervised learning finds patterns in data without any labels.
- **Examples**: Supervised learning is like having a teacher telling you which toy goes where, while unsupervised learning is like exploring and finding friends who like the same games as you.

Section 4: Fun Activities with Supervised and Unsupervised Learning

4.1 Label Your Toys!

Grab some toys and give them fun names. Can you teach a friend or a robot which toy is which? It's like being a teacher for a day!

4.2 Find Toy Friends!

Take a bunch of toys and see if you can group them into sets based on how they look or what they do. It's like being a detective and finding clues to solve a mystery!

Section 5: Real-World Fun with Machine Learning

5.1 Self-Driving Cars

Imagine a car that learns to drive itself by recognizing road signs and other cars. That's supervised learning in action!

5.2 Exploring New Music

Ever noticed how music apps suggest new songs you might like? They use unsupervised learning to find songs that sound similar to your favorites.

Section 6: Being a Good Data Scientist

6.1 Fair Play

It's important to use machine learning in fair ways. Sometimes, if the data isn't fair, the computer might make unfair decisions. As future data scientists, we can make sure everyone gets a fair chance.

6.2 Exploring Together

As you learn more about machine learning, remember to share your discoveries with friends. Together, you can explore and create cool things with what you've learned!

Section 7: Did You Know?

- Did you know computers can learn to play games like chess or even create artwork? They use supervised and unsupervised learning to become super smart!
- Unsupervised learning is like solving a puzzle without knowing what the picture will look like—it's all about finding patterns and making connections.

Section 8: Let's Recap!

Congratulations! You've finished Unit 2 on Supervised and Unsupervised Learning. Now you know how computers can learn from examples with labels and find hidden patterns on their own.

MODULE 6

Big Data and Data Engineering

UNIT 1

Introduction to Big Data Concepts and Technologies

Welcome to the world of Big Data, young data scientists! This module is all about understanding the vast universe of data we live in and how we can harness its power to make amazing discoveries and solve real-world problems. Get ready to explore the exciting concepts and technologies behind Big Data and Data Engineering!

Section 1: What is Big Data?

Imagine having a library so big that it contains every book ever written, every video ever made, and every song ever sung. That's what Big Data is like—a massive collection of information from all kinds of sources. But it's not just about size; Big Data is also about the variety and speed at which this information is generated.

1.1 The 3 Vs of Big Data

Let's break down Big Data into three main characteristics, known as the 3 Vs:

1. **Volume**: This is all about the sheer size of data. We're talking about terabytes, petabytes, and even exabytes of information. Think of all the videos uploaded to YouTube every minute or all the tweets sent every second. That's a lot of data!

2. **Velocity**: This is the speed at which data is created and processed. Imagine a rocketship zooming through space—that's how fast data is generated and needs to be analyzed. For example, streaming services like Netflix need to analyze viewing habits in real-time to recommend new shows.

3. **Variety**: This is the different types of data we have. It's not just text; it's images, videos, social media posts, sensor data, and more. Think about all the different kinds of information on your smartphone: photos, emails, fitness data, and so much more.

Section 2: Why is Big Data Important?

Big Data is like a treasure chest full of insights waiting to be discovered. By analyzing Big Data, we can uncover patterns, make predictions, and even change the world. Here are some ways Big Data is making a difference:

2.1 Healthcare

Imagine doctors predicting and preventing diseases before they even happen. By analyzing health data from millions of people, doctors can identify risk factors and develop new treatments. For example, wearable devices like smartwatches collect data about your heart rate and activity levels, helping doctors monitor your health in real-time.

2.2 Environment

Big Data helps us understand and protect our planet. By analyzing data from weather stations, satellites, and sensors, scientists can track climate change, predict natural disasters, and find ways to reduce pollution. For example, data from sensors placed in the ocean helps scientists monitor sea levels and protect marine life.

2.3 Business

Companies use Big Data to understand their customers and make better decisions. By analyzing data from social media, online purchases, and customer feedback, businesses can create personalized experiences and improve their products. For example, online retailers use Big Data to recommend products you might like based on your shopping history.

Section 3: Big Data Technologies

Handling Big Data requires powerful tools and technologies. Let's dive into some of the coolest technologies that make Big Data analysis possible:

3.1 Hadoop

Hadoop is like a super-sized storage and processing system for Big Data. It can handle huge amounts of data across many computers, making it perfect for big data tasks. Hadoop has two main parts:

1. **Hadoop Distributed File System (HDFS)**: This is the storage part. It splits large data files into smaller pieces and distributes them across many computers, ensuring data is stored safely and can be accessed quickly.
2. **MapReduce**: This is the processing part. It breaks down big data processing tasks into smaller tasks that can be done simultaneously across many computers, making it super-efficient.

Example: Analyzing Social Media Trends

Imagine you want to analyze millions of tweets to find out what people are saying about a new movie. Using Hadoop, you can store all those tweets in HDFS and then use MapReduce to process them, identifying popular keywords and trends in no time.

3.2 Spark

Apache Spark is like Hadoop's faster, cooler sibling. It's designed for lightning-fast data processing and can handle Big Data tasks that require quick, real-time analysis. Spark can work with Hadoop's HDFS, but it processes data much faster thanks to its in-memory computing.

Example: Real-Time Stock Market Analysis

Think about how stock markets need to analyze millions of trades every second. Using Spark, financial companies can process and analyze this data in real-time, making split-second decisions to buy or sell stocks based on current trends.

3.3 NoSQL Databases

Traditional databases (SQL) are great for structured data, but Big Data often includes unstructured data like social media posts and sensor data. That's where NoSQL databases come in. They can handle diverse data types and scale easily to accommodate massive amounts of information.

1. **MongoDB**: A document-based NoSQL database that's great for storing and querying large volumes of data with flexible, JSON-like documents.

   Example: Personalized Content Recommendations

   Websites like Netflix use MongoDB to store user profiles and viewing histories. By analyzing this data, they can recommend movies and TV shows tailored to each user's preferences.

2. **Cassandra**: A column-family NoSQL database designed for high availability and scalability, making it perfect for handling massive amounts of data across many servers.

   Example: Monitoring IoT Devices

   Smart home systems use Cassandra to store data from IoT devices like thermostats, lights, and security cameras. By analyzing this data, they can optimize energy usage and enhance home security.

Section 4: The Role of a Data Engineer

Data engineers are the architects of the Big Data world. They design, build, and maintain the systems that collect, store, and process massive amounts of data. Let's look at some key tasks they handle.

4.1 Data Collection

Data engineers collect data from various sources, such as social media, sensors, and online transactions. They use tools like Apache Kafka to handle data streams and ensure data is collected efficiently.

Example: Streaming Data from Wearable Devices

Think about how fitness trackers collect data on your steps, heart rate, and sleep patterns. Data engineers set up systems to stream this data from the devices to a central database, where it can be analyzed for insights into your health and fitness.

4.2 Data Storage

Storing Big Data requires systems that can handle vast amounts of information while ensuring it's accessible and secure. Data engineers use technologies like HDFS and cloud storage services like Amazon S3 to store data efficiently.

Example: Storing Customer Data for E-Commerce

Online stores collect data on millions of customers, including their browsing history, purchases, and preferences. Data engineers design storage systems to securely store this data, making it easy to access for personalized recommendations and marketing campaigns.

4.3 Data Processing

Processing Big Data involves transforming raw data into valuable insights. Data engineers use tools like Hadoop and Spark to process data, running complex algorithms and models to extract useful information.

Example: Analyzing Traffic Patterns

Cities collect data from traffic cameras and sensors to monitor traffic flow and congestion. Data engineers set up systems to process this data in real-time, helping city planners optimize traffic lights and reduce congestion.

4.4 Data Pipeline

A data pipeline is like a factory assembly line for data. It involves collecting, processing, and moving data from one place to another. Data engineers design and manage these pipelines to ensure data flows smoothly and efficiently.

Example: Delivering News Feeds

News websites collect data from various sources, like articles, videos, and social media. Data engineers create pipelines to aggregate this data, process it for relevance, and deliver personalized news feeds to readers.

Section 5: Challenges in Big Data

Working with Big Data isn't always easy. There are several challenges data engineers face when handling massive amounts of data.

5.1 Data Quality

Ensuring data is accurate, complete, and consistent is crucial. Poor data quality can lead to incorrect insights and decisions.

Example: Cleaning Healthcare Data

Hospitals collect data from different sources, like patient records and medical devices. Data engineers must ensure this data is accurate and consistent to support effective treatments and research.

5.2 Scalability

Big Data systems need to scale to handle increasing amounts of data. Data engineers design systems that can grow and adapt as data volumes increase.

Example: Scaling Social Media Platforms

Social media platforms like Facebook and Twitter handle billions of posts, likes, and comments daily. Data engineers design scalable systems to manage this massive influx of data and ensure the platforms run smoothly.

5.3 Security

Protecting sensitive data from unauthorized access and breaches is critical. Data engineers implement security measures to safeguard data and ensure compliance with regulations.

Example: Securing Financial Data

Banks handle sensitive financial information, like transaction records and account details. Data engineers design systems with robust security measures to protect this data from cyber threats and ensure customer privacy.

Section 6: Ethics in Big Data

With great data comes great responsibility. As data scientists and engineers, it's important to use Big Data ethically and responsibly.

6.1 Privacy

Respecting user privacy is essential. Ensure data is collected and used in ways that protect individuals' privacy and comply with regulations.

Example:

When analyzing customer data, companies can anonymize personal information to protect privacy while still gaining valuable insights.

6.2 Transparency

Be transparent about how data is collected, used, and shared. Users should know what data is being collected and how it's being used.

Example: Transparent Data Practices

Tech companies can provide clear privacy policies and allow users to control their data settings, ensuring transparency and trust.

6.3 Fairness

Ensure data and algorithms are free from bias and do not discriminate against any group. Strive for fairness and equality in all data practices.

Example: Fairness in Hiring Algorithms

Companies using AI for hiring should ensure their algorithms are free from bias, promoting fair and equal opportunities for all candidates.

Section 7: Let's Recap!

Congratulations, data explorers! You've completed Unit 1 on Big Data Concepts and Technologies. Now, you understand what Big Data is, why it's important, and the amazing technologies and challenges involved in working with it. You're well on your way to becoming a Big Data expert!

Stay tuned for Unit 2, where we'll dive deeper into Data Engineering and learn how to design and build robust data systems. Keep exploring, experimenting, and having fun with Big Data. The future of data science is bright, and it's yours to shape.

This unit has introduced the concepts and technologies of Big Data in a fun and engaging way. By blending real-world examples with practical activities and ethical considerations, we hope to inspire you to explore further and discover the incredible potential of Big Data and Data Engineering.

UNIT 2

Understanding data storage and retrieval systems

Welcome back, future data wizards! In Unit 1, we dived into the vast universe of Big Data and explored some cool technologies that make sense of it all. Now, we're going to embark on another adventure: understanding how data is stored and retrieved. This might sound a bit like organizing a giant library, but trust us, its way cooler and packed with tech magic. Ready? Let's go!

Section 1: Why Data Storage and Retrieval Matter

Imagine you have a room filled with millions of books, toys, and gadgets. Without a system to store and find things, it would be chaos! The same goes for Big Data. Efficient data storage and retrieval systems ensure that all the information we collect is organized, secure, and easily accessible when needed.

1.1 The Basics of Data Storage

At its core, data storage is about keeping data safe and accessible. It involves saving data in a structured way so that it can be retrieved and used whenever required. This includes:

- **Storing**: Saving data in databases, file systems, or other storage mediums.
- **Organizing**: Structuring data so that it's easy to search and retrieve.
- **Securing**: Protecting data from unauthorized access and ensuring privacy.
- **Maintaining**: Keeping data safe from corruption or loss over time.

1.2 The Basics of Data Retrieval

Data retrieval is all about finding and accessing the stored data efficiently. Think of it as having a super-speedy librarian who can find any book you need in a flash. Data retrieval involves:

- **Querying**: Asking the system to find specific data.
- **Indexing**: Creating a system to quickly locate data.
- **Fetching**: Retrieving the data from storage and presenting it to the user.

Section 2: Types of Data Storage Systems

Just like we have different ways to store things at home—like shelves for books and boxes for toys—there are various data storage systems suited for different kinds of data. Let's explore some of the most popular ones.

2.1 Relational Databases (SQL)

Relational databases are like the neat and tidy bookshelves of the data world. They store data in tables, where each table has rows and columns. Each row is a record, and each column is a field with a specific type of data (like names, dates, or numbers).

Example: A School Database

Imagine a database for a school that stores information about students, teachers, and classes.

- **Students Table**: Each row represents a student, with columns for name, age, grade, and student ID.
- **Teachers Table**: Each row represents a teacher, with columns for name, subject, and teacher ID.
- **Classes Table**: Each row represents a class, with columns for class name, teacher ID, and student IDs.

Relational databases use Structured Query Language (SQL) to manage and query data. Here are some popular relational databases:

- **MySQL**: An open-source database known for its reliability and performance.
- **PostgreSQL**: Another open-source database, famous for its advanced features and support for complex queries.
- **SQLite**: A lightweight, file-based database that's great for mobile apps and small projects.

2.2 NoSQL Databases

NoSQL databases are the wild, fun, and flexible cousins of relational databases. They're designed to handle a wide variety of data types and structures, making them perfect for Big Data applications.

Example: A Social Media App

Imagine a social media app that stores posts, comments, likes, and user profiles. The data is varied and doesn't fit neatly into tables. NoSQL databases can handle this with ease.

Types of NoSQL Databases:

- **Document Databases**: Store data as documents (often in JSON format). Examples include MongoDB and CouchDB.

  Example: A user profile might be stored as a JSON document with fields for name, age, bio, and a list of posts.

- **Key-Value Stores**: Store data as key-value pairs, like a giant dictionary. Examples include Redis and DynamoDB.

  Example: A session store where the key is a session ID and the value is user-specific data.

- **Column-Family Stores**: Store data in columns rather than rows. Examples include Cassandra and HBase.

  Example: A table where each row represents a user, and columns store various attributes like user ID, name, and recent activities.

- **Graph Databases**: Store data as nodes and relationships, perfect for networks. Examples include Neo4j and OrientDB.

    Example: A social network where nodes are users and relationships are friendships or follows.

2.3 File Storage Systems

Sometimes, data doesn't fit into databases and is better stored as files. File storage systems manage and organize these files.

Example: Cloud Storage

Think about how you use services like Google Drive or Dropbox to store photos, documents, and videos. These services use file storage systems to manage your data.

Types of File Storage Systems:

- **Local File Systems**: Store files on a single computer or server. Examples include NTFS (Windows) and ext4 (Linux).

    Example: Your computer's hard drive where you store personal documents and photos.

- **Distributed File Systems**: Store files across multiple computers or servers. Examples include HDFS (Hadoop Distributed File System) and Amazon S3.

    Example: Big data analytics platforms use HDFS to store massive datasets across many servers.

Section 3: Data Retrieval Techniques

Now that we know how data is stored, let's explore how we can retrieve it efficiently. Retrieving data involves searching, indexing, and querying techniques.

3.1 Query Languages

Query languages are the tools we use to ask databases for specific data. Just like you might ask a librarian to find a book by title or author, you use query languages to find data in a database.

Example: SQL Queries

- **SELECT**: Fetches data from a table.

```
SELECT * FROM Students WHERE grade = 'A';
```

- **INSERT**: Adds new data to a table.

```
INSERT INTO Students (name, age, grade) VALUES ('Alice', 14, 'A');
```

- **UPDATE**: Changes existing data in a table.

```
UPDATE Students SET grade = 'B' WHERE name = 'Alice';
```

- **DELETE**: Removes data from a table.

```
DELETE FROM Students WHERE name = 'Alice';
```

3.2 Indexing

Indexing is like creating a map or a shortcut to quickly find data. It's used to speed up search queries by reducing the amount of data the system needs to scan.

Example: Indexing in a Library

Imagine a library where books are indexed by title, author, and subject. Instead of searching every shelf, you can use the index to find the exact location of a book.

- **Primary Index**: Created on a table's primary key (unique identifier).

    Example: An index on the student ID in the Students table.

- **Secondary Index**: Created on non-primary key columns to speed up specific queries.

    Example: An index on the grade column to quickly find students with a specific grade.

3.3 Caching

Caching is like keeping frequently used data in a quick-access drawer, so you don't have to fetch it from the storage system every time.

Example: Web Browser Cache

Your web browser caches images and web pages you visit frequently, so they load faster the next time you visit them.

Types of Caches:

- **In-Memory Caches**: Store data in RAM for super-fast access. Examples include Redis and Memcached.

    Example: A website might use Redis to cache user session data, speeding up access to frequently used information.

- **Content Delivery Networks (CDNs)**: Cache web content like images and videos on servers around the world to speed up delivery to users.

     Example: Streaming services use CDNs to deliver videos to users quickly, regardless of their location.

Section 4: Challenges in Data Storage and Retrieval

Storing and retrieving Big Data is no easy task. There are several challenges data engineers face:

4.1 Scalability

As data grows, storage and retrieval systems must scale to handle the increased load. This involves adding more storage capacity and ensuring the system can process more data efficiently.

Example: Scaling an E-Commerce Platform

An online store collects data on millions of transactions and customer interactions. As the store grows, its data storage and retrieval systems must scale to handle the increased data volume and ensure fast access for personalized shopping experiences.

4.2 Data Consistency

Ensuring that data remains consistent across different storage systems is crucial. This means that all users and applications see the same data, even when changes are made.

Example: Online Banking

When you transfer money between accounts, it's essential that the transaction is reflected accurately in your account balance. Data engineers ensure consistency by using techniques like distributed transactions and consensus algorithms.

4.3 Data Security

Protecting data from unauthorized access and breaches is critical. This involves implementing security measures like encryption, access controls, and monitoring.

Example: Securing Personal Data

Social media platforms collect and store vast amounts of personal data. Data engineers implement security measures to protect this data from hackers and ensure user privacy.

Section 5: Ethics in Data Storage and Retrieval

With great data comes great responsibility. As data scientists and engineers, it's important to handle data ethically and responsibly:

5.1 Privacy

Respecting user privacy is essential. Ensure data is stored and retrieved in ways that protect individuals' privacy and comply with regulations.

Example: Anonymizing Data

When storing and analyzing customer data, anonymize personal information to protect privacy while still gaining valuable insights.

5.2 Transparency

Be transparent about how data is stored, used, and shared. Users should know what data is being collected and how it's being used.

Example: Transparent Data Policies

Tech companies can provide clear data storage policies and allow users to control their data settings, ensuring transparency and trust.

5.3 Security

Implement robust security measures to protect data from unauthorized access and breaches. This includes encryption, access controls, and monitoring.

Example: Securing Health Records

Healthcare providers store sensitive patient information. Data engineers implement strong security measures to protect this data from cyber threats and ensure patient privacy.

Section 6: Let's Recap!

Congratulations, data adventurers! You've completed Unit 2 on Data Storage and Retrieval Systems. Now, you understand the different types of storage systems, how to efficiently retrieve data, and the challenges involved in managing Big Data.

UNIT 3

Exploring Distributed Computing Frameworks like Hadoop and Spark

Welcome back, data explorers! We've journeyed through the vast landscapes of Big Data, understanding its concepts and how to store and retrieve it efficiently. Now, it's time to unleash the power of distributed computing frameworks that make handling Big Data not just manageable, but downright awesome. Get ready to dive into the worlds of Hadoop and Spark, two superhero frameworks that bring Big Data to life. Let's go!

Section 1: What is Distributed Computing?

Before we meet our superheroes, let's understand what distributed computing is all about. Imagine you have a ginormous task, like counting all the stars in the sky. Doing it alone would take forever! But what if you had thousands of friends helping you count simultaneously? That's the essence of distributed computing: breaking a huge task into smaller chunks and solving them across multiple computers at the same time.

1.1 How Distributed Computing Works

Distributed computing involves:

- **Dividing a Task**: Splitting a large task into smaller, manageable pieces.
- **Distributing the Task**: Assigning each piece to a different computer (or node) in a network.
- **Processing in Parallel**: Each node works on its piece of the task simultaneously.
- **Combining Results**: Gathering and combining the results from all nodes to get the final output.

Example: Baking Cookies

Imagine you need to bake 10,000 cookies for a giant bake sale. Doing it alone would be overwhelming! But if you had 10 friends, each baking 1,000 cookies in their own kitchen at the same time, you'd get the job done much faster. Distributed computing is like having a team of bakers working in parallel to achieve a common goal.

Section 2: Introducing Hadoop

Meet Hadoop, our first Big Data superhero! Hadoop is an open-source framework designed to store and process massive amounts of data across a cluster of computers. It's like the ultimate team captain, coordinating tasks and ensuring everything runs smoothly.

2.1 The Hadoop Ecosystem

The Hadoop ecosystem consists of several components, each with a specific role. Let's meet the main players:

- **HDFS (Hadoop Distributed File System)**: The storage system of Hadoop, designed to handle large files by splitting them into smaller blocks and distributing them across the cluster.

- **MapReduce**: The processing engine of Hadoop, which breaks down tasks into small pieces, processes them in parallel, and combines the results.

- **YARN (Yet Another Resource Negotiator)**: Manages resources and schedules tasks across the Hadoop cluster.

- **HBase**: A NoSQL database that runs on top of HDFS, providing real-time read/write access to large datasets.

Example: The Ultimate Team Captain

Imagine you're organizing a giant charity event. You have different teams handling food, decorations, entertainment, and logistics. Hadoop is like the team captain, ensuring everyone knows their tasks, coordinates their efforts, and everything runs smoothly.

2.2 How Hadoop Works

Let's break down how Hadoop handles a Big Data task, like analyzing a massive dataset of social media posts to find trending topics.

- **Data Storage with HDFS**: The dataset is split into smaller blocks and stored across multiple nodes in the HDFS. Each block is replicated across nodes for fault tolerance.

- **Processing with MapReduce**: The analysis task is broken down into smaller tasks using MapReduce. Each node processes its portion of the data, and the results are combined to identify trending topics.

- **Resource Management with YARN**: YARN manages the resources and schedules the tasks to ensure efficient processing.

Section 3: Introducing Spark

Now, meet Spark, our next Big Data superhero! Spark is another open-source framework designed for fast and flexible data processing. It's like Hadoop's speedy sidekick, capable of handling both batch and real-time data processing with ease.

3.1 The Spark Ecosystem

Spark's ecosystem is rich with components designed for various data processing tasks:

- **Spark Core**: The engine that provides the foundation for all Spark components, handling basic I/O functionalities.

- **Spark SQL**: Allows querying of structured data using SQL, making it easy to work with data frames and tables.

- **Spark Streaming**: Enables real-time processing of streaming data, such as live social media feeds or sensor data.

- **MLlib**: A machine learning library with scalable algorithms for classification, regression, clustering, and more.

- **GraphX**: A library for graph processing, enabling analysis of social networks, web graphs, and more.

Example: The Speedy Sidekick

Imagine you're a superhero duo fighting crime. Hadoop is the strategist, planning and coordinating large operations, while Spark is the speedy sidekick, quickly responding to real-time threats and handling complex tasks with agility.

3.2 How Spark Works

Let's explore how Spark handles a Big Data task, like analyzing real-time sensor data from a smart city to detect anomalies.

- **Data Storage**: Spark can work with data stored in HDFS, databases, or cloud storage services.

- **Data Processing**: Spark processes data in-memory, making it incredibly fast. It can handle batch processing for historical data and real-time streaming data simultaneously.

- **Machine Learning with MLlib**: Spark's MLlib can be used to train models on historical data and apply them to streaming data to detect anomalies in real-time.

Section 4: Comparing Hadoop and Spark

Now that we've met Hadoop and Spark, let's compare these two superheroes to understand their strengths and when to use each one.

4.1 Speed and Performance

- **Hadoop**: Designed for batch processing, Hadoop is reliable but can be slower because it writes intermediate results to disk.

- **Spark**: Spark is designed for in-memory processing, making it much faster than Hadoop, especially for iterative algorithms and real-time data processing.

Example: Speedy Sidekick vs. Strategic Captain

Hadoop is like a strategic captain who carefully plans and executes tasks, ensuring everything is done correctly. Spark is like a speedy sidekick who can quickly handle real-time tasks and respond to immediate threats.

4.2 Ease of Use

- **Hadoop**: Requires writing complex MapReduce code for data processing tasks.

- **Spark**: Provides high-level APIs in Java, Scala, Python, and R, making it easier to write and maintain code.

Example: Coding Wizards

Using Hadoop's MapReduce can feel like casting a complex spell with many steps. Spark's high-level APIs are like using a magic wand, where a few swishes and flicks (lines of code) do the trick.

4.3 Flexibility

- **Hadoop:** Primarily designed for batch processing and works well with unstructured data.

- **Spark:** Highly flexible, capable of handling batch processing, real-time streaming, machine learning, and graph processing.

Example: The Versatile Hero

Spark is like a versatile hero who can handle multiple types of challenges, from fighting crime in real-time to solving complex mysteries with historical data.

Section 5: Real-World Applications

Both Hadoop and Spark are used by companies around the world to tackle Big Data challenges. Let's explore some real-world applications to see these frameworks in action.

5.1 E-Commerce and Recommendation Systems

- **Hadoop**: E-commerce giants use Hadoop to process massive amounts of transaction data and generate personalized recommendations for customers.

- **Spark**: Companies use Spark's MLlib to build real-time recommendation systems that analyze customer behavior and suggest products instantly.

Example: Shopping Assistant

Imagine you're shopping online, and the site recommends items you might like based on your past purchases. Hadoop processes the historical data, and Spark analyzes your real-time browsing behavior to suggest the perfect items.

5.2 Social Media Analytics

- **Hadoop**: Social media platforms use Hadoop to store and process vast amounts of user-generated content, analyzing trends and user sentiment.

- **Spark**: Spark Streaming is used to analyze live social media feeds, detecting trending topics and real-time user interactions.

Example: Trend Detector

Think of a social media platform that highlights trending topics. Hadoop crunches the historical data to understand long-term trends, while Spark Streaming monitors live feeds to detect what's trending right now.

5.3 Healthcare and Medical Research

- **Hadoop**: Healthcare providers use Hadoop to store and analyze patient records, medical images, and research data.

- **Spark**: Spark's MLlib helps researchers build predictive models for disease outbreaks and personalized treatment plans based on real-time patient data.

Example: Health Guardian

Imagine a system that predicts flu outbreaks based on patient data. Hadoop stores and processes historical data, while Spark analyzes live data from hospitals and clinics to provide real-time predictions and alerts.

Section 6: Challenges in Distributed Computing

Working with distributed computing frameworks like Hadoop and Spark comes with its own set of challenges. Let's explore some of these and how data engineers overcome them.

6.1 Data Distribution and Fault Tolerance

Ensuring data is evenly distributed across nodes and handling node failures gracefully is crucial.

- **Hadoop**: HDFS replicates data across multiple nodes to ensure fault tolerance.

- **Spark**: Spark's RDDs (Resilient Distributed Datasets) are designed to recover from node failures and continue processing.

Example: Backup Plan

Imagine a team of bakers with backup ovens. If one oven fails, the bakers can continue using the remaining ovens to ensure the cookies are baked on time.

6.2 Resource Management

Efficiently managing resources to avoid bottlenecks and ensure optimal performance is essential.

- **Hadoop**: YARN manages resources and schedules tasks across the Hadoop cluster.

- **Spark**: Spark's dynamic resource allocation adjusts resource usage based on the workload.

Example: Efficient Team Management

Think of a sports team where the coach allocates players based on the game strategy. Efficient resource management ensures each player (or node) is used optimally for the best performance.

6.3 Scalability

As data grows, the system must scale to handle increased load without compromising performance.

- **Hadoop**: Designed to scale horizontally by adding more nodes to the cluster.

- **Spark**: Spark's in-memory processing and support for distributed computing make it highly scalable.

Example: Expanding the Kitchen

Imagine you need to bake more cookies as demand increases. Adding more bakers and ovens (scaling horizontally) ensures you can meet the growing demand without delays.

Section 8: Let's Recap!

Awesome job, data adventurers! You've explored the exciting worlds of Hadoop and Spark, learning how these distributed computing frameworks handle Big Data tasks efficiently and effectively.

Stay tuned for more adventures in Big Data and Data Engineering. Keep exploring, experimenting, and having fun with Hadoop and Spark. The future of data science is bright, and it's yours to shape!

This unit has introduced the concepts and technologies of distributed computing frameworks like Hadoop and Spark in a fun and engaging way. By blending real-world examples with practical activities and ethical considerations, we hope to inspire you to explore further and discover the incredible potential of Big Data and Data Engineering.

MODULE 7

Ethical Considerations in Data Science

UNIT 1

Discussing ethical considerations in data collection and analysis

Welcome back, data detectives! As we continue our journey through the vast world of data science, it's crucial to remember that with great data power comes great responsibility. Today, we're diving into the realm of ethics in data science. We'll explore the ethical considerations you need to keep in mind when collecting and analyzing data. Let's embark on this mission to become not just skilled data scientists, but ethical ones too!

Section 1: Why Ethics Matter in Data Science

Before we get into the nitty-gritty, let's understand why ethics is such a big deal in data science. Imagine you have a magic wand that lets you see and analyze everything. Cool, right? But what if you use it to invade people's privacy or make unfair decisions? Not so cool anymore. That's where ethics come in – they help us use our data powers responsibly.

1.1 Defining Ethics

Ethics are the moral principles that govern our behavior. In data science, ethics guide us on how to handle data respectfully, responsibly, and fairly.

Example: The Golden Rule

Think about the golden rule: treat others as you want to be treated. In data science, it means handling others' data as carefully as you'd want your data to be handled.

1.2 The Impact of Unethical Data Practices

Unethical data practices can lead to serious consequences, such as:

Privacy Violations: Unauthorized access to personal data can harm individuals.

Bias and Discrimination: Unfair algorithms can reinforce societal biases.

Loss of Trust: Once trust is broken, it's hard to regain, affecting both individuals and organizations.

Example: The Data Scandal

Remember the major data breaches and scandals where companies misused personal data? They not only caused public outrage but also led to legal repercussions and a loss of trust.

Section 2: Ethical Considerations in Data Collection

Collecting data ethically is the first step towards responsible data science. Let's explore the key ethical considerations you need to keep in mind when gathering data.

2.1 Informed Consent

Informed consent means getting permission from individuals before collecting their data. People should know what data is being collected, why, and how it will be used.

Example: The Survey

Imagine you're conducting a survey on favorite ice cream flavors. You need to inform participants about the survey's purpose and get their consent before they share their tasty preferences.

2.2 Anonymity and Confidentiality

Respecting anonymity and confidentiality means protecting the identities and personal information of individuals.

Example: Anonymous Poll

Suppose you're running a school election poll. Ensure the votes are anonymous so students feel comfortable voting honestly without fear of their choices being exposed.

2.3 Data Minimization

Data minimization involves collecting only the data you truly need for your analysis, nothing more.

Example: The Minimalist Shopper

Think of yourself as a minimalist shopper, buying only what you need. When collecting data, focus on gathering only the essential information to achieve your goals.

Section 3: Ethical Considerations in Data Analysis

Once you've collected data ethically, the next step is to analyze it responsibly. Here are the key ethical considerations during data analysis.

3.1 Avoiding Bias

Bias in data analysis can lead to unfair and inaccurate results. It's crucial to identify and minimize biases in your data and algorithms.

Example: The Fair Judge

Imagine you're a judge at a talent show. To be fair, you need to evaluate each performance without any preconceived notions or biases. The same principle applies to data analysis.

3.2 Ensuring Transparency

Transparency means being open about your data sources, methods, and algorithms. It helps build trust and allows others to understand and replicate your work.

Example: The Transparent Chef

Imagine a chef who shares their recipes openly, so others can understand and replicate their delicious dishes. Similarly, being transparent in your data analysis builds trust and credibility.

3.3 Accountability

Accountability means taking responsibility for your data and analysis. If something goes wrong, own up to it and take steps to correct it.

Example: The Responsible Captain

Think of yourself as the captain of a ship. If the ship faces trouble, you take responsibility and navigate it to safety. In data science, being accountable means addressing issues and ensuring accurate results.

Section 4: Real-World Scenarios and Ethical Dilemmas

Let's dive into some real-world scenarios and ethical dilemmas that data scientists might face. Understanding these situations will help you navigate the complex world of data ethics.

4.1 Scenario 1: The Social Media Analysis

You've been hired to analyze social media data to identify trends and improve marketing strategies. But the data includes personal information and private messages.

Ethical Consideration: Ensure you have consent to use the data and anonymize personal information to protect privacy.

Example: The Privacy Protector

Imagine you're a guardian of a magical library with secret diaries. You can read the diaries to understand trends, but you must protect the identities of the writers to maintain their trust.

4.2 Scenario 2: The Hiring Algorithm

You're developing an algorithm to help a company with hiring decisions. However, the training data includes biases against certain groups.

Ethical Consideration: Identify and remove biases from the data to ensure fair and unbiased hiring practices.

Example: The Fair Recruiter

Think of yourself as a recruiter who wants to hire the best candidates without any bias. You ensure the hiring process is fair for everyone, regardless of their background.

4.3 Scenario 3: The Health Data Study

You're conducting a study using health data to find patterns in disease outbreaks. The data includes sensitive medical information.

Ethical Consideration: Obtain informed consent, anonymize the data, and ensure it's used only for the intended purpose.

Example: The Ethical Doctor

Imagine you're a doctor conducting a study to improve public health. You handle patients' data with the utmost care, respecting their privacy and consent.

Section 5: Ethical Frameworks and Guidelines

To help you navigate ethical considerations, there are several frameworks and guidelines you can follow. These provide a structured approach to ethical decision-making in data science.

5.1 The FAIR Data Principles

The FAIR principles emphasize making data Findable, Accessible, Interoperable, and Reusable. Following these principles ensures that data is handled responsibly and transparently.

Example: The Librarian

Imagine you're a librarian organizing a library. The FAIR principles help you ensure that books (data) are easy to find, accessible to everyone, and can be used by different systems and readers.

5.2 The Five Safes Framework

The Five Safes framework provides guidelines for safe data usage, focusing on safe projects, people, data, settings, and outputs.

Example: The Safety Inspector

Think of yourself as a safety inspector ensuring that data projects, people handling data, data itself, settings where data is used, and outputs from data analysis are all safe and secure.

5.3 Data Ethics Canvas

The Data Ethics Canvas is a tool to help you think through the ethical implications of your data projects. It covers aspects like data collection, storage, analysis, sharing, and use.

Example: The Ethical Planner

Imagine you're planning a big event, considering every detail to ensure it runs smoothly and ethically. The Data Ethics Canvas helps you plan your data projects with the same level of detail and ethical consideration.

Section 6: Let's Recap!

Awesome work, data detectives! You've explored the fascinating world of ethics in data science, understanding how to collect and analyze data responsibly. By considering informed consent, anonymity, bias, transparency, and accountability, you're well on your way to becoming an ethical data scientist.

Remember, ethics isn't just a set of rules – it's about making thoughtful decisions that respect individuals and society. As you continue your data science journey, keep these ethical principles in mind and strive to use your data powers for good. The future of data science is in your hands, and together, we can make it ethical and awesome!

This unit has delved into the critical ethical considerations in data collection and analysis, providing you with the knowledge and tools to navigate the ethical landscape of data science. By blending real-world examples, practical activities, and ethical frameworks, we hope to inspire you to become not only skilled data scientists but also responsible and ethical ones.

UNIT 2

Understanding bias and fairness in machine learning models

Let's delve into a topic that's super important in the world of data science: bias and fairness in machine learning models. Imagine you're designing a game, and it always favors one player over the others. Unfair, right? That's exactly what happens when machine learning models are biased. They can end up making decisions that aren't fair, which can have serious real-world consequences. Our mission today is to understand what bias is, how it sneaks into our models, and how we can make sure our models play fair. Let's get started!

Section 1: What is Bias in Machine Learning?

Bias in machine learning refers to the tendency of a model to make systematic errors. These errors can come from the data we use to train the model or from the way the model is designed.

1.1 Types of Bias

Selection Bias: This happens when the data we use to train our model doesn't represent the real world. If certain groups are left out or overrepresented, our model learns from an incomplete picture.

Example: Selection Bias

Imagine you're building a model to predict who will enjoy a new video game. If you only use data from players in one country, your model might not work well for players from other countries because it hasn't learned about their preferences.

Measurement Bias: This occurs when there are errors in how data is collected. If our measurements are off, the data won't accurately reflect reality.

Example: Measurement Bias

Suppose you're training a fitness app that tracks steps, but the app's sensors work better on certain types of shoes. The data collected would be biased, affecting the accuracy of the step counts.

Algorithmic Bias: This happens when the design of the algorithm introduces bias. The assumptions we make when building the model can lead to biased outcomes.

Example: Algorithmic Bias

Consider an algorithm designed to filter job applications. If it prioritizes certain keywords that are more common in applications from a specific demographic, it might favor that group over others.

1.2 Understanding Fairness

Fairness in machine learning is about ensuring that our models treat all individuals or groups equitably. There are several ways to define fairness:

Equal Opportunity: Ensuring that the model gives equal chances of positive outcomes to all groups.

Demographic Parity: Ensuring that the model's predictions are equally distributed across different groups.

Fairness Through Unawareness: Building models without considering sensitive attributes like race, gender, or age.

Example: Fairness in Credit Scoring

Imagine a model used to assess creditworthiness. Ensuring fairness means that people from different racial backgrounds have equal chances of receiving credit. The model shouldn't unfairly favor one group over another.

Section 2: Sources of Bias in Machine Learning

Bias can sneak into machine learning models from various sources. Let's explore some common sources and how they impact the fairness of our models.

2.1 Data Collection and Representation

The data we collect forms the foundation of our machine learning models. If the data is biased, our model will likely be biased too.

Historical Bias: When historical data reflects existing societal biases, the model trained on such data will learn and perpetuate these biases.

Example: Imagine training a hiring algorithm using historical data from a company where most employees are men. The model might learn to favor male candidates, reflecting the historical bias present in the data.

Sampling Bias: This occurs when the data sample isn't representative of the population, leading to skewed results.

Example: Suppose you're building a health prediction model but only use data from young, healthy individuals. The model might not work well for older adults or those with chronic conditions.

2.2 Labeling and Annotation

How we label and annotate our data can introduce bias. If the labeling process is subjective, it can lead to biased outcomes.

Human Bias: When human annotators bring their own biases into the labeling process.

Example: Suppose you're building a sentiment analysis model to understand movie reviews. If human annotators have a bias towards certain genres, they might label reviews inconsistently, affecting the model's performance.

Ambiguity in Labels: When labels are ambiguous or inconsistent, leading to biased training data.

Example: Imagine annotators labeling customer reviews as positive or negative. If there's no clear guideline, one annotator might label a mildly satisfied review as positive, while another might label it as negative.

2.3 Algorithm Design

The design of the algorithm itself can introduce bias. The assumptions and choices made during model development play a crucial role in the fairness of the final model.

Bias in Objective Functions: The objective function that the algorithm optimizes might not consider fairness.

Example: Consider a recommendation system that prioritizes user engagement. If it's designed to maximize clicks, it might end up recommending sensational content that isn't fair or balanced.

Feature Selection: Including or excluding certain features can introduce bias.

Example: Imagine building a model to predict job performance. If you include features like "college attended" and it turns out certain colleges are predominantly attended by specific groups, the model might favor those groups, introducing bias.

Section 3: Detecting Bias in Machine Learning Models

Detecting bias in machine learning models is the first step towards addressing it. Here are some techniques and tools you can use to identify bias in your models.

3.1 Analyzing Model Performance Across Groups

One way to detect bias is to analyze the model's performance across different demographic groups. If the model performs significantly better or worse for certain groups, it might be biased.

Performance Metrics: Use metrics like accuracy, precision, recall, and F1-score to compare model performance across groups.

Example: Suppose you have a facial recognition model. By evaluating its accuracy across different skin tones, you might discover that the model performs worse for darker skin tones, indicating bias.

Confusion Matrix: Analyze the confusion matrix for different groups to understand where the model makes errors.

Example: In a loan approval model, analyzing confusion matrices for different income groups might reveal that the model is more likely to incorrectly reject applications from lower-income applicants.

3.2 Fairness Metrics

There are specific fairness metrics you can use to detect bias in your models:

Demographic Parity: Measures if the positive prediction rate is the same across different groups.

Equal Opportunity: Measures if the true positive rate is the same across different groups.

Disparate Impact: Measures the ratio of positive outcomes between different groups.

Example: For a loan approval model, you can use demographic parity to check if approval rates are similar across different racial groups. If there's a significant disparity, the model might be biased.

3.3 Bias Auditing Tools

Several tools can help you detect and visualize bias in your machine learning models:

AI Fairness 360: An open-source toolkit by IBM that provides metrics and algorithms to detect and mitigate bias.

Fairness Indicators: A tool by Google that provides metrics for evaluating fairness in machine learning models.

Example: You're developing a hiring model and use AI Fairness 360 to audit it. The tool helps you identify that the model favors candidates from certain universities, allowing you to take corrective action.

Section 4: Mitigating Bias in Machine Learning Models

Once you've detected bias in your model, the next step is to mitigate it. Here are some strategies and techniques to ensure your models are fair and unbiased.

4.1 Pre-Processing Techniques

Pre-processing techniques involve modifying the training data to reduce bias before feeding it into the model.

Re-sampling: Balancing the dataset by oversampling underrepresented groups or undersampling overrepresented groups.

Example: Imagine you're training a model to predict student success and realize that data from certain schools is underrepresented. By oversampling data from those schools, you can create a more balanced dataset.

Data Augmentation: Adding synthetic data to balance the dataset.

Example: In a facial recognition dataset, you might generate additional images of underrepresented groups to ensure the model learns to recognize all faces equally well.

De-biasing Data: Removing or transforming biased data features.

Example: For a hiring model, you might remove names and other identifying information from resumes to prevent the model from learning biased patterns based on these features.

4.2 In-Processing Techniques

In-processing techniques involve modifying the learning algorithm to reduce bias during training.

Fairness Constraints: Incorporating fairness constraints into the model's objective function.

Example: You're developing a credit scoring model and incorporate fairness constraints to ensure the model's predictions do not favor any particular group.

Adversarial Debiasing: Training the model with an adversarial network that penalizes biased predictions.

Example: You're building a hiring model and use adversarial debiasing to ensure the model doesn't favor any gender. This approach helps create a more balanced and fair model.

4.3 Post-Processing Techniques

Post-processing techniques involve modifying the model's outputs to ensure fairness after training.

Threshold Adjustment: Adjusting decision thresholds for different groups to ensure fair outcomes.

Example: Consider a medical diagnosis model that predicts the likelihood of a disease. By adjusting the decision threshold for different demographic groups, you can ensure fairer diagnostic outcomes.

Equalized Odds Post-Processing: Modifying the model's predictions to ensure equalized odds across groups.

Example: You have a loan approval model and modify its predictions so that the true positive rate and false positive rate are similar across all demographic groups, ensuring fairness.

Section 5: Let's Recap!

You've explored the fascinating world of bias and fairness in machine learning, understanding how bias creeps into our models and how we can ensure they are fair and just. By considering data collection, algorithm design, and fairness metrics, you're well on your way to becoming an ethical data scientist.

Remember, fairness isn't just a box to check – it's about making thoughtful decisions that promote equity and justice. As you continue your data science journey, keep these principles in mind and strive to create models that are fair and unbiased. The future of ethical AI is in your hands, and together, we can make it equitable and awesome!

UNIT 3

Encouraging Responsible Use of Data and Algorithms

As budding data scientists, it's crucial to recognize the immense responsibility that comes with handling data and designing algorithms. Responsible use of data involves ensuring privacy, transparency, and fairness in all stages of data collection, processing, and analysis. This means obtaining informed consent from data subjects, anonymizing sensitive information, and minimizing data collection to only what is necessary. Transparency is about making our processes and models understandable to others, documenting methodologies clearly, and openly communicating how decisions are made. Fairness requires us to actively seek and mitigate biases in our datasets and models, ensuring that our algorithms treat all individuals and groups equitably. By adhering to these principles, we build trust, promote ethical practices, and contribute positively to society.

Moreover, accountability and societal impact are fundamental aspects of responsible data science. Accountability involves regularly auditing our models, being receptive to feedback, and taking responsibility for any adverse outcomes. It's important to understand the legal and ethical frameworks guiding our work, ensuring compliance with data protection laws and ethical guidelines. Considering the broader societal impact means anticipating the long-term effects of our algorithms and striving to use our data powers for social good. Education, continuous learning, and interdisciplinary collaboration play vital roles in enhancing our understanding of ethical data practices. By fostering a culture of responsibility within our organizations and among our peers, we can ensure that our work not only advances technological progress but also promotes justice, equity, and the well-being of all communities.

MODULE 8

QUIZ TIME

Welcome to the quiz game, data detectives! Get ready to test your knowledge with some fun and engaging multiple-choice questions (MCQs). Don't worry; we'll go over the answers once you've completed all the questions. Good luck!

1. What is machine learning?

- A) Teaching machines to play sports
- B) A type of artificial intelligence that allows computers to learn from data
- C) A programming language
- D) A video game

2. In supervised learning, what do we use to train the model?

- A) Unlabeled data
- B) Labeled data
- C) Random numbers
- D) Music files

3. Which of these is an example of supervised learning?

- A) Clustering
- B) Regression
- C) Dimensionality reduction
- D) Data cleaning

4. What is unsupervised learning?

- A) Learning without a teacher
- B) Learning with labeled data
- C) Learning with unlabeled data
- D) Learning from books

5. Which of the following is a common use case for unsupervised learning?

- A) Predicting stock prices
- B) Classifying emails as spam or not spam
- C) Clustering similar items
- D) Predicting house prices

6. What is Big Data?

- A) A large number of small files
- B) Extremely large datasets that traditional data processing software can't handle
- C) A type of social media
- D) A programming language

7. Which of these is a characteristic of Big Data?

- A) Volume
- B) Velocity
- C) Variety
- D) All of the above

8. What does data engineering focus on?

- A) Building machine learning models
- B) Designing data storage and retrieval systems
- C) Creating video games
- D) Writing novels

9. Which technology is commonly associated with Big Data storage and processing?

- A) Hadoop
- B) Photoshop
- C) Microsoft Word
- D) Excel

10. What is the purpose of Apache Spark?

- A) Designing websites
- B) Data processing and analytics
- C) Creating graphics
- D) Writing essays

11. What is a data lake?

- A) A lake filled with data
- B) A storage repository that holds a vast amount of raw data
- C) A type of data visualization tool
- D) A programming language

12. What does a NoSQL database offer compared to a traditional relational database?

- A) More colors
- B) Greater scalability and flexibility for certain types of data
- C) Faster internet speeds
- D) Better sound quality

13. Why is data privacy important?

- A) To keep secrets from friends
- B) To protect individuals' personal information
- C) To make data colorful
- D) To confuse hackers

14. What is data anonymization?

- A) Making data funny
- B) Removing personally identifiable information from data
- C) Writing data backwards
- D) Encrypting data

15. What does transparency mean in the context of data science?

- A) Making data invisible
- B) Being open about how data and algorithms are used
- C) Encrypting data
- D) Cleaning data

16. Which of these is a fairness principle in data science?

- A) Always using the same data
- B) Ensuring algorithms treat all individuals equitably
- C) Keeping algorithms secret
- D) Using colorful charts

17. What is algorithmic accountability?

- A) Blaming the computer for mistakes
- B) Taking responsibility for the outcomes of your algorithms
- C) Hiding your code from others
- D) Playing games on the computer

18. What is the role of a data engineer?

- A) Building machine learning models
- B) Designing and maintaining data systems
- C) Painting artwork

- D) Playing video games

19. Which of the following is an ethical consideration in data collection?

- A) Collecting as much data as possible
- B) Ensuring data collection respects privacy and consent
- C) Making data look interesting
- D) Hiding data from others

20. Why is it important to consider the societal impact of data and algorithms?

- A) To impress friends
- B) To promote social good and prevent harm
- C) To win awards
- D) To make data colorful

21. What is data integrity?

- A) Keeping data honest
- B) Ensuring data is accurate and consistent
- C) Making data colorful
- D) Hiding data from others

22. What is a common challenge in Big Data?

- A) Running out of ideas
- B) Managing and processing large volumes of data efficiently
- C) Making data look pretty
- D) Writing long essays

23. What is a distributed computing framework?

- A) A structure for organizing office furniture
- B) A system that allows processing of large data sets across multiple computers
- C) A new type of laptop
- D) A game for coding

24. Which of the following is a tool used for data visualization?

- A) Hadoop
- B) Power BI
- C) Spark
- D) HDFS

25. What does "ETL" stand for in data engineering?

- A) Enter, Track, Load
- B) Extract, Transform, Load

- C) Eat, Travel, Learn
- D) Entertain, Teach, Laugh

26. What is the primary focus of data analysis?

- A) Making data colorful
- B) Extracting meaningful insights from data
- C) Collecting data
- D) Encrypting data

27. Why is education important for promoting responsible data use?

- A) To confuse competitors
- B) To ensure data scientists are aware of ethical considerations and best practices
- C) To increase data volume
- D) To make data look nice

28. What is "data ethics"?

- A) Following rules for organizing files
- B) Ensuring data is used in morally good ways
- C) Writing code neatly
- D) Collecting as much data as possible

29. What is the main goal of ethical data science?

- A) To build the fastest algorithms
- B) To ensure data and algorithms are used in ways that are fair, transparent, and respectful of privacy
- C) To collect as much data as possible
- D) To hide data from others

30. What is "real-time data processing"?

- A) Processing data instantly as it is received
- B) Processing data after a week
- C) Processing data next year
- D) Delaying data processing

ANSWERS

1. B) A type of artificial intelligence that allows computers to learn from data
2. B) Labeled data
3. B) Regression
4. C) Learning with unlabeled data
5. C) Clustering similar items
6. B) Extremely large datasets that traditional data processing software can't handle
7. D) All of the above
8. B) Designing data storage and retrieval systems
9. A) Hadoop
10. B) Data processing and analytics
11. B) A storage repository that holds a vast amount of raw data
12. B) Greater scalability and flexibility for certain types of data
13. B) To protect individuals' personal information
14. B) Removing personally identifiable information from data
15. B) Being open about how data and algorithms are used
16. B) Ensuring algorithms treat all individuals equitably
17. B) Taking responsibility for the outcomes of your algorithms
18. B) Designing and maintaining data systems
19. B) Ensuring data collection respects privacy and consent
20. B) To promote social good and prevent harm
21. B) Ensuring data is accurate and consistent
22. B) Managing and processing large volumes of data efficiently
23. B) A system that allows processing of large data sets across multiple computers
24. B) Power BI
25. B) Extract, Transform, Load
26. B) Extracting meaningful insights from data
27. B) To ensure data scientists are aware of ethical considerations and best practices
28. B) Ensuring data is used in morally good ways
29. B) To ensure data and algorithms are used in ways that are fair, transparent, and respectful of privacy
30. A) Processing data instantly as it is received

MODULE 9

The Historical Evolution of Data Science: Milestones, Influential Figures, & Breakthroughs

Introduction

The field of data science has emerged as a pivotal discipline in the modern era, revolutionizing how we collect, analyze, and derive insights from data. Spanning multiple domains—from statistics and computer science to domain-specific applications—data science has a rich and intricate history shaped by technological advancements, theoretical developments, and the growing importance of data-driven decision-making. This narrative explores the historical context of data science, highlighting key milestones, influential figures, and breakthroughs that have shaped its evolution over time.

Early Beginnings: Foundations in Statistics and Mathematics

The roots of data science can be traced back to the early 20th century, where pioneers in statistics laid the groundwork for understanding and analyzing data. One of the seminal figures during this period was Ronald Fisher, a British statistician whose work on experimental design, analysis of variance (ANOVA), and statistical hypothesis testing provided fundamental principles that underpin modern data analysis. Fisher's contributions not only formalized statistical methods but also emphasized the importance of rigorous experimentation and data-driven decision-making in scientific research.

In the 1940s and 1950s, the advent of computers marked a significant turning point in data processing and analysis. Early computers, such as the ENIAC (Electronic Numerical Integrator and Computer), enabled researchers to perform complex calculations and process large volumes of data more efficiently than ever before. This era laid the groundwork for computational statistics, as researchers began to explore how computers could automate and enhance statistical analysis techniques.

Emergence of Data Mining and Machine Learning

The 1960s and 1970s witnessed the emergence of data mining and machine learning as distinct fields within data science. One of the pioneering figures during this period was John Tukey, an American mathematician and statistician who coined the term "bit" and made significant contributions to exploratory data analysis (EDA). Tukey's approach emphasized visualizing data to uncover patterns and insights—an approach that remains foundational in modern data science practice.

In parallel, researchers began developing early machine learning algorithms aimed at teaching computers to learn from data and make predictions. Arthur Samuel's work on the Samuel Checkers-playing Program in the late 1950s exemplified early efforts in machine learning, demonstrating how computers could be trained to improve their performance through experience. This laid the groundwork for the development of neural networks and other advanced machine learning techniques in subsequent decades.

The Data Explosion and Rise of Big Data

The late 20th and early 21st centuries marked a profound shift in the landscape of data science with the advent of the internet, digital technologies, and the proliferation of data-generating devices. The exponential growth of data—commonly referred to as "big data"—posed new challenges and opportunities for data scientists. Researchers and practitioners were tasked with developing new methods and tools to store, process, and analyze vast amounts of data in real-time.

One of the key milestones during this period was the development of Apache Hadoop in the mid-2000s. Hadoop, an open-source framework designed for distributed storage and processing of large datasets, revolutionized big data analytics by enabling scalable and cost-effective data processing across clusters of computers. Hadoop's MapReduce programming model, coupled with the Hadoop Distributed File System (HDFS), provided a foundation for building scalable data processing applications and fueled advancements in data-driven decision-making across industries.

Rise of Data Science as a Discipline

The early 21st century witnessed the formalization and recognition of data science as a distinct discipline encompassing elements of statistics, computer science, and domain expertise. Organizations began to recognize the strategic importance of data-driven insights in gaining competitive advantage, driving innovation, and informing decision-making. This led to a growing demand for skilled data scientists capable of extracting actionable insights from complex datasets.

In academia, institutions started offering specialized programs and degrees in data science, aimed at equipping students with the necessary skills in statistical analysis, machine learning, data visualization, and data management. The interdisciplinary nature of data science encouraged collaboration across disciplines, fostering new research areas such as data ethics, privacy-preserving techniques, and explainable AI.

Breakthroughs in Artificial Intelligence and Deep Learning

The resurgence of artificial intelligence (AI) and the development of deep learning techniques in the 2010s marked another pivotal moment in the evolution of data science. Deep learning, a subfield of machine learning inspired by the structure and function of the human brain, revolutionized tasks such as image recognition, natural language processing, and speech recognition. Breakthroughs in deep learning algorithms, particularly convolutional neural networks (CNNs) and recurrent neural networks (RNNs), enabled unprecedented levels of accuracy and performance in handling complex and unstructured data.

One of the landmark achievements in deep learning was the ImageNet Challenge in 2012, where a deep learning model called AlexNet significantly outperformed traditional computer vision approaches. This milestone demonstrated the transformative potential of deep learning in real-world applications and spurred investments in AI research and development across academia and industry.

Ethical Considerations and Responsible Data Science

As data science continued to advance, so too did concerns about ethical implications, privacy risks, and biases inherent in data-driven technologies. Ethical considerations in data science became increasingly prominent, prompting discussions around fairness, transparency, and accountability in algorithmic decision-making. Researchers and practitioners began exploring methods for mitigating biases, ensuring data privacy, and fostering responsible data practices.

In response to these challenges, frameworks such as the General Data Protection Regulation (GDPR) in Europe and initiatives like the Responsible AI movement emerged to promote ethical standards and guidelines for the responsible use of data and AI technologies. These efforts underscored the importance of interdisciplinary collaboration, stakeholder engagement, and continuous education in addressing ethical dilemmas and societal impacts associated with data science.

Future Directions and Emerging Trends

Looking ahead, the field of data science continues to evolve rapidly, driven by advancements in AI, machine learning, and computational technologies. Emerging trends such as federated learning, quantum computing, and the Internet of Things (IoT) present new opportunities and challenges for data scientists, offering innovative solutions to complex problems across various domains.

The integration of data science with other disciplines—such as biology, healthcare, finance, and social sciences—promises to unlock new insights and transformative applications in personalized medicine, financial forecasting, urban planning, and social policy. Moreover, the democratization of data science tools and platforms enables broader participation and empowers individuals and organizations to harness the power of data for innovation and societal good.

Conclusion

In conclusion, the historical evolution of data science reflects a journey of innovation, collaboration, and transformative impact across multiple domains. From its foundations in statistics and mathematics to the advent of big data, machine learning, and deep learning, data science has reshaped how we understand, interpret, and utilize data to solve complex problems and drive informed decision-making.

As we navigate the future landscape of data science, ethical considerations, interdisciplinary collaboration, and responsible data practices will continue to be paramount. By embracing these principles and leveraging cutting-edge technologies, data scientists can contribute to advancing knowledge, addressing global challenges, and creating a more inclusive and sustainable future.

The journey of data science is far from over, and the next chapter promises to be as exciting and transformative as those that have come before.

MODULE 10

Fun Facts

Data is everywhere: Every minute, we create an enormous amount of data—more than 500 hours of video are uploaded to YouTube, and around 188 million emails are sent every minute!

The Term "Data Scientist" is Relatively New: The term "data scientist" was first coined in 2008 by DJ Patil and Jeff Hammerbacher while working at LinkedIn and Facebook, respectively.

Big Data's Big Beginnings: The concept of big data dates back to the 1940s when the US census was first stored on punched cards and then processed by an early computer.

Machine Learning at Play: Netflix uses machine learning to recommend shows you might like based on your watching habits. It's like having a personal TV assistant!

AI Artists: There are AI programs that can create paintings, write music, and even compose poetry. Some AI-generated art has been sold for thousands of dollars!

Data for the Environment: Data scientists are using data from satellites and sensors to help protect endangered species and monitor climate change.

Personal Assistants: Virtual assistants like Siri, Alexa, and Google Assistant use data science to understand and respond to your voice commands.

Health Data Saves Lives: Data science helps in predicting disease outbreaks, understanding genetic disorders, and personalizing medical treatments.

Sporting Data: Sports teams use data science to analyze players' performances, strategize games, and even scout new talent.

Social Media Insights: Platforms like Instagram and Twitter analyze data from millions of users to show you trending topics and suggest new friends.

Music Recommendations: Services like Spotify and Apple Music use algorithms to recommend songs based on your listening history. It's why your playlists keep getting better!

Google's PageRank: Google's famous search algorithm, PageRank, which revolutionized internet searching, is a product of data science.

AI in Games: Video game developers use AI to create smarter non-player characters (NPCs) that learn and adapt to players' actions.

Fighting Crime: Police departments use data analysis to predict crime hotspots and deploy resources more effectively.

Astronomy and Data: Data scientists help astronomers analyze massive datasets from telescopes to discover new planets and stars.

Retail Magic: Retailers use data science to understand customer preferences, manage inventory, and optimize the layout of their stores.

Self-Driving Cars: Autonomous vehicles use data from sensors and cameras to navigate streets, avoid obstacles, and follow traffic laws.

Agriculture and Data: Farmers use data science to monitor soil conditions, forecast weather, and manage crops more efficiently.

Language Translation: Apps like Google Translate use machine learning to provide real-time translations in multiple languages.

Predicting Movies' Success: Movie studios use data analysis to predict which movies will be box office hits based on factors like cast, genre, and historical data.

Predictive Text: Your phone's keyboard uses data science to predict what word you're going to type next. That's why your texts can almost read your mind!

Facebook Friend Suggestions: Facebook uses data science to suggest people you may know based on mutual friends, schools, workplaces, and other connections.

Gaming Stats: Online multiplayer games use data to match you with players of similar skill levels, ensuring balanced and fun gameplay.

Weather Forecasting: Meteorologists use data from satellites, radars, and sensors to predict weather conditions, helping people prepare for storms and other events.

Shopping Ads: Ever noticed how online ads seem to know what you like? E-commerce websites use your browsing data to show personalized advertisements.

DNA Sequencing: Data science is crucial in genomics for sequencing DNA, helping scientists understand genetic diseases and develop treatments.

Sentiment Analysis: Companies use data science to analyze social media posts and reviews to gauge public sentiment about their products and services.

Recommendation Engines: Amazon uses data science to recommend products you might like based on your past purchases and browsing history.

Real-time Translation: Google's real-time language translation for text and speech relies heavily on data science and machine learning.

Movie Recommendations: Streaming services like Netflix use data science to analyze viewing habits and suggest movies and shows you might enjoy.

Bank Fraud Detection: Banks use data science to detect fraudulent transactions by identifying unusual patterns in spending behavior.

Urban Planning: Cities use data science to analyze traffic patterns, optimize public transportation routes, and improve infrastructure planning.

Health Monitoring: Wearable devices like fitness trackers collect and analyze health data to help you monitor your activity levels and overall health.

Crop Yield Prediction: Farmers use data science to predict crop yields, optimize planting schedules, and improve agricultural efficiency.

Smart Homes: Smart home devices use data to learn your habits and preferences, adjusting lighting, temperature, and even music to suit your mood.

Space Exploration: NASA uses data science to analyze data from space missions, helping scientists understand our universe better.

Virtual Reality: Data science helps create immersive virtual reality experiences by analyzing user movements and adjusting the virtual environment in real-time.

Airline Pricing: Airlines use data science to dynamically adjust ticket prices based on demand, booking patterns, and other factors.

Energy Management: Utility companies use data to predict energy usage patterns and manage supply to prevent outages and reduce costs.

Customer Service Chatbots: Many websites use AI-powered chatbots to provide customer service, answering questions, and solving problems using data science.

Fashion Trends: Fashion brands use data science to analyze trends and predict which styles will be popular in the coming seasons.

Personalized Learning: Educational platforms use data to create personalized learning experiences, adapting to each student's strengths and weaknesses.

Music Discovery: Music streaming services analyze listening habits to help you discover new artists and genres you might like.

Election Predictions: Data scientists analyze polling data and other factors to predict election outcomes.

Smart Traffic Lights: Some cities use data to optimize traffic light timing, reducing congestion and improving traffic flow.

Online Dating: Dating apps use data science to match users based on their preferences, behavior, and interests.

Voice Assistants: Voice recognition technologies used in Siri, Alexa, and Google Assistant rely on data science to understand and respond to commands.

Disease Outbreak Prediction: Data scientists analyze health data to predict and track disease outbreaks, helping to prevent epidemics.

Retail Analytics: Stores analyze sales data to determine the best product placement and inventory levels, optimizing the shopping experience.

Video Streaming Quality: Streaming services use data science to adjust video quality based on your internet connection, ensuring a smooth viewing experience.

STORY TIME

The Data Detective

A Fictional Adventure in Data Science

Chapter 1: The Infotropolis Enigma

In the bustling metropolis of Infotropolis, a city renowned for its technological advancements and digital prowess, lived a young and brilliant data detective named Ada. Ada wasn't your typical detective with a magnifying glass and trench coat; she wielded algorithms, data visualization tools, and a relentless curiosity about the patterns and secrets hidden within data.

Ada's office was a hub of activity, filled with the hum of computers and the glow of multiple screens. Her team included Max, a prodigious coder with a penchant for ethical hacking, and Zoe, a data analyst whose keen eye could turn raw numbers into meaningful stories. Together, they tackled the city's most perplexing data-related mysteries.

One crisp morning, as Ada was sipping her coffee and perusing her latest predictive model, she received an urgent call from Mayor Thompson. The city's central database, the heart of Infotropolis' smart city infrastructure, had been compromised.

Vital data was disappearing, and if not resolved quickly, the city's essential services could grind to a halt.

Chapter 2: The Initial Investigation

Ada and her team sprang into action, heading straight to the Infotropolis Data Center. They were greeted by Mr. Perez, the head engineer, who explained that the data had started vanishing mysteriously over the past week. Despite their best efforts, they couldn't pinpoint the source of the breach.

In the control room, walls lined with monitors displayed real-time data flows and system health indicators. Max immediately got to work, writing scripts to parse through the immense logs for any unusual activity. Zoe began visualizing the data patterns over time, seeking anomalies that could provide clues.

As the hours ticked by, Ada noticed a curious pattern. The data wasn't just randomly disappearing; it was being meticulously targeted. Sensitive information, crucial for the city's operation, was being deleted with precision. This required not just technical skill but intimate knowledge of the database's architecture.

Chapter 3: Setting the Trap

Realizing they were dealing with a highly skilled adversary, Ada decided to set a trap. Max crafted a decoy database filled with fake but plausible data, making it appear as if it contained highly sensitive information. The team hoped this would lure the hacker into making a mistake.

Late one night, their trap was sprung. The decoy database showed signs of unauthorized access. Max's alarm system immediately flagged the intrusion, and he traced the hacker's location to an abandoned warehouse on the outskirts of Infotropolis.

Armed with this information, Ada, Max, and Zoe headed to the warehouse. The building was dark and silent, a stark contrast to the city's vibrant core. Inside, they found a dimly lit room filled with computer equipment. At the center sat a young woman, furiously typing away at her keyboard. She looked up, startled as they entered.

Chapter 4: The Hacker's Confession

"It's over," Ada said calmly. "We know what you've been doing."

The woman, who introduced herself as Lyra, confessed. She was a former employee of the data center, let go during budget cuts. Feeling betrayed and desperate, she decided to sabotage the city's data systems to prove her worth and demand her job back.

As Lyra explained her actions, Ada couldn't help but feel a mix of anger and sympathy. Lyra was clearly talented but had made poor choices. Ada knew that while Lyra had to face consequences, there was also a chance for redemption.

Ada proposed a deal to Mayor Thompson: Lyra would work with the city to improve their data security systems, using her skills for good. In return, she would receive a lighter sentence and a chance to make amends.

Chapter 5: Rebuilding and Improving

With Lyra's insider knowledge and Ada's guidance, they not only restored the missing data but also enhanced the security of the city's databases. Infotropolis was soon back on track, and its operations ran smoother than ever before.

As part of Ada's team, Lyra found a new purpose. She dedicated herself to protecting the city's data and ensuring such breaches wouldn't happen again. Ada, Max, and Zoe welcomed her, recognizing that everyone deserves a second chance to make things right.

Chapter 6: The Quantum Conundrum

Just as the team settled into their improved routines, a new challenge arose. Infotropolis had recently invested in a cutting-edge quantum computer, promising to revolutionize data processing with its unparalleled speed. However, strange anomalies began to occur in the quantum data outputs, leading to bizarre and inexplicable results.

Mayor Thompson, impressed by Ada's previous success, called on her team once more. Ada, intrigued by the mysteries of quantum computing, eagerly accepted the challenge. She and her team dived into the world of qubits, superposition, and entanglement, seeking to understand the root cause of the anomalies.

Working closely with Dr. Elena Martinez, a quantum physicist, they discovered that a rival city, Technotropolis, had been conducting unauthorized experiments on the quantum network. These experiments were causing interference, leading to the strange data anomalies.

Chapter 7: The Quantum Showdown

Determined to put an end to Technotropolis's meddling, Ada devised a plan. Max would create a secure quantum firewall to protect Infotropolis's data, while Zoe analyzed the patterns of interference to predict Technotropolis's next move. Ada herself would confront the rival city's officials, presenting evidence of their unauthorized activities.

The showdown was intense. Technotropolis initially denied any wrongdoing, but the irrefutable data presented by Ada's team forced them to back down. They agreed to cease their experiments and collaborate with Infotropolis on quantum research, ensuring mutual benefit and scientific advancement.

Chapter 8: A City Transformed

With the quantum crisis averted, Infotropolis continued to thrive. The collaborative efforts with Technotropolis led to groundbreaking discoveries in quantum computing, benefiting both cities. Ada's team became renowned for their expertise and ethical approach to data science, attracting talent and projects from around the world.

Lyra, now fully integrated into the team, played a pivotal role in these advancements. Her unique perspective and skills proved invaluable, turning her from a rogue hacker into a respected data scientist.

Chapter 9: The Ethical Evolution

Throughout their adventures, Ada emphasized the importance of ethical data usage. She initiated city-wide workshops and educational programs, teaching citizens and budding data scientists about the responsible handling of data. The city's motto, "Data for Good," became a guiding principle, influencing policies and practices across various sectors.

Ada's commitment to ethics inspired many, including young students who saw data science not just as a career, but as a tool for positive change. The city's culture shifted towards greater transparency and accountability, ensuring that data was used to enhance the quality of life for all residents.

Chapter 10: The Future Beckons

As the sun set over Infotropolis, Ada stood on the balcony of her office, reflecting on their journey. From the mystery of the disappearing data to the quantum conundrum, they had faced numerous challenges and emerged stronger each time.

Max and Zoe joined her, and together they marveled at the city they had helped shape. Infotropolis was not just a hub of technological innovation; it was a beacon of ethical data use and collaboration.

"We've come a long way," Max said, gazing at the skyline.

"And we've still got a long way to go," Ada replied with a smile. "There are always new mysteries to solve and new frontiers to explore."

As the city lights twinkled in the dusk, the team knew that their work was far from over. The world of data science was vast and ever-changing, and they were ready for whatever challenges lay ahead.

Epilogue: Legacy of the Data Detectives

Years later, Infotropolis stood as a model city, admired globally for its innovative use of data and technology. The Infotropolis Data Science Institute, founded by Ada and her team, became a premier center for research and education, attracting the brightest minds from around the world.

Ada's team continued to push the boundaries of what was possible, tackling global challenges such as climate change, public health, and cybersecurity with their unparalleled expertise. Their adventures were chronicled in books and documentaries, inspiring future generations to pursue careers in data science and uphold the highest ethical standards.

And so, the legacy of the Data Detectives lived on, a testament to the power of curiosity, collaboration, and the responsible use of data. Infotropolis thrived, and with it, the hope that data science could indeed make the world a better place.

Potential Breakthroughs

Here are some potential breakthroughs in data science that scientists are currently working on or may explore in the future:

- **Explainable AI (XAI):** Researchers are focusing on developing AI models that not only provide accurate predictions but also offer explanations for their decisions. XAI aims to enhance transparency, trustworthiness, and accountability in AI systems, making them more accessible and interpretable for users and stakeholders.

- **Federated Learning:** This emerging technique allows multiple parties to collaboratively train machine learning models without sharing their private data. Federated learning preserves data privacy and security while enabling collective learning across distributed devices, such as smartphones and IoT devices.

- **AI Ethics and Bias Mitigation:** There is a growing emphasis on addressing ethical considerations and biases in AI and machine learning algorithms. Researchers are exploring methods to mitigate biases, ensure fairness, and uphold ethical standards in algorithmic decision-making across diverse applications and domains.

- **Quantum Machine Learning:** Integrating quantum computing principles with machine learning algorithms holds promise for solving complex optimization problems and enhancing the efficiency of AI computations. Quantum machine learning may lead to breakthroughs in areas such as drug discovery, materials science, and cryptography.

- **Generative AI Models:** Advances in generative models, such as Generative Adversarial Networks (GANs) and Variational Autoencoders (VAEs), are enabling computers to create realistic synthetic data, images, and text. Future applications include virtual prototyping, creative industries, and personalized content generation.

- **Graph Neural Networks (GNNs):** GNNs are specialized neural networks designed to process and analyze structured data represented as graphs. Researchers are exploring applications of GNNs in social networks, recommendation systems, drug discovery, and understanding complex relationships in data.

- **AI-driven Personalization and Adaptation:** Future developments may focus on AI systems that adapt dynamically to individual preferences, behaviors, and contexts in real-time. Personalized AI could transform industries such as healthcare, education, and retail by delivering tailored experiences and recommendations.

- **Responsible AI Development:** There is a growing movement towards developing AI systems that prioritize ethical considerations, user privacy, and societal well-being. Researchers and organizations are advocating for frameworks and guidelines to ensure responsible AI deployment and governance.

- **Multi-modal AI:** Integrating multiple sources of data, such as text, images, audio, and video, into cohesive AI models enables more comprehensive and nuanced understanding of complex phenomena. Multi-modal AI could revolutionize fields like multimedia analysis, autonomous vehicles, and augmented reality.

- **Continual Learning and Adaptation:** AI systems capable of continual learning and adaptation in dynamic environments are a focus of ongoing research. These systems can acquire new knowledge, refine existing models, and adapt to changing conditions without requiring retraining from scratch.

- **Augmented Intelligence**: Enhancing human decision-making and creativity through AI-driven insights and recommendations, blending human intuition with machine intelligence.

- **Causal Inference:** Advancements in causal modeling and inference techniques to understand cause-and-effect relationships from observational and experimental data.

- **Robust AI:** Developing AI systems that are resilient to adversarial attacks, noise, and anomalies, ensuring reliability and security in real-world applications.

- **AI for Sustainability:** Leveraging AI and data science to address environmental challenges, optimize resource allocation, and promote sustainable practices in industries such as agriculture, energy, and urban planning.

- **Neuromorphic Computing:** Designing AI systems inspired by the human brain's neural architecture, enabling efficient processing of sensory data and complex pattern recognition tasks.

- **Edge Computing and AI:** Deploying AI models directly on edge devices (e.g., smartphones, IoT sensors) to enable real-time processing, reduce latency, and preserve data privacy.

- **Interpretable Machine Learning:** Developing methods to interpret and visualize how machine learning models arrive at their decisions, enhancing trust and accountability in AI systems.

- **AI-driven Drug Discovery:** Accelerating the discovery and development of new pharmaceuticals through AI-driven predictive modeling, virtual screening, and molecular design.

- **Digital Twins:** Creating virtual replicas of physical systems or processes using real-time data and simulations, facilitating predictive maintenance, optimization, and innovation in various industries.

- **AI in Social Good:** Harnessing AI for social impact, including applications in healthcare accessibility, disaster response, poverty alleviation, and education equity.

These breakthroughs in data science have the potential to reshape industries, drive innovation, and address global challenges in ways that were previously unimaginable. As researchers continue to push the boundaries of what is possible, the future of data science holds exciting possibilities for improving our understanding of the world and enhancing the human experience.

Glossary

Here's a glossary of terms related to the topics covered in our discussions:

- **Data Science:** The interdisciplinary field that uses scientific methods, processes, algorithms, and systems to extract knowledge and insights from structured and unstructured data.
- **Machine Learning:** A subset of artificial intelligence (AI) that enables systems to learn from data and improve their performance over time without being explicitly programmed.
- **Supervised Learning:** A type of machine learning where the algorithm learns from labeled data, making predictions or decisions based on past data.
- **Unsupervised Learning:** A type of machine learning where the algorithm learns from unlabeled data, discovering patterns and structures without specific guidance.
- **Big Data:** Large and complex datasets that are difficult to manage and process using traditional data processing applications.
- **Data Engineering:** The discipline of designing, building, and maintaining the systems and architectures that enable the collection, storage, and processing of data.
- **Data Storage:** The process of storing data in different types of databases, file systems, or cloud storage solutions for easy retrieval and management.
- **Data Retrieval:** The process of accessing and extracting stored data from databases or other data storage systems.
- **Distributed Computing:** A model in which multiple computers work together to solve a single problem or perform a task, often used in big data processing.
- **Hadoop:** An open-source framework that allows for the distributed processing of large datasets across clusters of computers using simple programming models.
- **Spark:** An open-source unified analytics engine for large-scale data processing, providing high-level APIs in Java, Scala, Python, and R.
- **Ethical Considerations:** The moral principles and guidelines that govern the responsible collection, use, and sharing of data to avoid harm and ensure fairness.
- **Bias in Machine Learning:** Systematic errors or inaccuracies in machine learning algorithms that result in unfair outcomes, often due to skewed training data.
- **Fairness in Machine Learning:** The goal of ensuring that machine learning models do not discriminate against individuals or groups based on sensitive attributes such as race or gender.
- **Responsible Use of Data:** Practices and policies that promote transparency, accountability, and ethical behavior in the collection, analysis, and application of data.

- **Quantum Computing:** A type of computing that takes advantage of quantum-mechanical phenomena, such as superposition and entanglement, to perform operations on data.
- **Virtual Reality (VR):** A computer-generated simulation of a three-dimensional environment that can be interacted with in a seemingly real or physical way by a person using special electronic equipment.
- **Artificial Intelligence (AI):** The simulation of human intelligence processes by machines, especially computer systems.
- **Internet of Things (IoT):** The network of physical devices, vehicles, home appliances, and other items embedded with electronics, software, sensors, actuators, and connectivity which enables these objects to connect and exchange data.
- **Blockchain:** A decentralized and distributed digital ledger that records transactions across many computers in such a way that the registered transactions cannot be altered retroactively.

Conclusion

As we reach the end of our journey through the fascinating realms of data science, machine learning, and big data, it's important to reflect on how far you've come and the incredible potential that lies ahead. You've ventured into the intricate world of algorithms, discovered the power of data to reveal hidden patterns, and understood the profound ethical considerations that come with handling information responsibly. The topics we've covered—from the basics of machine learning and the magic of supervised and unsupervised learning to the vast expanses of big data technologies and the critical importance of data ethics—have equipped you with a foundational understanding that is both empowering and exciting. Remember, this is just the beginning. The field of data science is ever-evolving, with new discoveries and advancements unfolding every day. Your curiosity and dedication to learning will be your greatest allies as you navigate this dynamic landscape.

As you move forward, consider how you can apply these skills and knowledge in real-world scenarios. Whether you're analyzing trends for a school project, creating innovative apps, or simply exploring data for fun, the tools and concepts you've learned will be invaluable. Embrace challenges as opportunities to grow, and don't be afraid to experiment and ask questions. The beauty of data science lies in its ability to transform abstract numbers into meaningful insights that can drive change and innovation. Stay mindful of the ethical implications of your work, striving always to use data in ways that are fair, transparent, and beneficial to society. The world of data science is vast and full of possibilities, and you are now equipped with the keys to explore it. Keep learning, stay curious, and remember that every great discovery begins with a single question. Congratulations on completing this journey, and here's to many more exciting adventures in the world of data!